The Klein Method Of Early Reading Mastery

A New Model for Teaching Young Children to Read

Ages 3-7

Teaching Children How to Teach Themselves to Read

Randall Klein

Book Design by HMDpublishing

Contents

Part I: A New Model for Teaching Young Children to Read

Part II: Implementing the Method

PART I

A New Model for Teaching Young Children to Read

Introduction

This instruction manual is a careful explanation of the method and materials of a new model of early reading instruction for beginning and struggling readers ages 3-7 years. This method is ideal for early childhood classrooms but also very effective as an intervention program for students who have fallen behind in the early grades.

The activities in this program give beginning and struggling readers a concrete understanding of the alphabetic principle, strong letter knowledge, confident decoding, and fluent word identification.

This new model of teaching young children to read gives students, teachers, and parents a well-defined sequence of self-guided learning activities leading to early reading success.

It is a new model because it provides children movement and hands-on learning, choice, self-motivation, and repetition—all vital elements of early learning and good instruction.

Perhaps more importantly the Klein Method allows children to share in the responsibility for their own learning.

Self-Guided Learning

Children to a great extent teach themselves to read. We can't possibly teach them all the phonics and spelling rules they need to decode words they've never read before containing letter combinations they haven't learned. Many children somehow figure it out on their own. But there are far too many who don't. This method helps *all* children "figure it out."

The Klein Method of Early Reading Mastery guides children to teach themselves the sounds of letters and how to decode simple, short words and then more complex words with unfamiliar spelling patterns and letter combinations.

This method teaches children how to teach themselves, and provides the games and activities that activate this self-guided learning.

Stated differently, this method teaches children *how* to teach themselves, and it provides games and activities that activate this self-guided learning.

This simple alphabet card illustrates an example of a self-guided activity. When a child learns to isolate the beginning sound of the word GOAT (*/g/*), he can then identify the sound of that abstract symbol next to the goat. Once we teach a child how this sound-symbol relationship works, we don't need to tell him the sound of a letter—if there is a key picture next to that letter. He can begin to teach *himself*.

The child who can tell me that the letter "g" makes the sound /g/ doesn't necessarily *know* that letter yet. He may not remember it tomorrow or even five minutes from now. But the child clearly recognizes the relationship between the picture and the letter and is now able to play games that direct him to match sounds to letters.

Sound & Letter Sorting

This Sound & Letter Sorting activity is based on the child's ability to isolate the beginning sound of a picture, which then guides him to choose the letter that matches that sound.

You don't need to tell the child the sound of a letter if there is a key picture next to that letter.

By matching sounds to symbols using interesting and fun hands-on learning games the child will easily learn those printed letters as *sounds*. Not through memorization, but through the work of his own hands and by repeated opportunity to match concrete sounds to abstract symbols. This is *self-directed* learning. It is an application of the *alphabetic principle.*

The Alphabetic Principle

The alphabetic principle is the relationship between sound and symbol—that printed letters represent the sounds of spoken language. When you match sounds to letters you are applying the alphabetic principle. Applying the alphabetic principle is the most effective way for a child to gain knowledge and mastery of these sound-symbol associations, or what we call phonics.

Teach the alphabetic principle before you teach the alphabet.

Our guiding principle is to *teach the alphabetic principle before you teach the alphabet.*

Each alphabet and decoding activity in this book involves the matching of sounds to symbols, of speech to print. Instead of asking a child to read a letter or decode a word—which is really a *test*, a kind of final exam—the games direct the child to choose printed letters or words that *match* the sounds of a spoken word depicted by an image.

Beginning Sounds & letters

For example, when a child can isolate the beginning sound of the word HOUSE, he can easily find the letter that matches that sound. And the sound of that letter is reinforced by the child's own activity.

When a child can isolate all three of the sounds of the word FAN, he can easily find the word with the letters that match those sounds. Also, by matching sounds to letters the child will experience what it will feel like to decode, because this matching process mimics what it sounds like to decode.

3-Letter Word Choice

The application of the alphabetic principle to identify letters and words is the basis of all the activities in this method and it is how the child will teach himself to read.

A New Role for the Teacher

A teacher who implements this method will play a new role in the learning environment, very different from a traditional role that focuses on direct, group instruction. After organizing the games and activities in the recommended manner, the teacher's role is to facilitate the learning process and supervise practice sessions. Key to this new role is teaching children to share in the responsibility for their own learning.

The teacher will show the children how they can take charge of the work of learning to read. The responsibility for practicing skills and choosing the correct materials gradually shifts from teacher to student. This is accomplished through the way games and activities are organized in the environment and the use of *self-checking practice sheets*. (See Appendix C.)

Activity Clusters

Students gain mastery of the foundational skills of phonemic awareness, letter recognition and decoding through meaningful practice with hands-on activities that are organized in easy-to-identify activity clusters. Each cluster matches a specific skill or set of skills.

The *Activities with Sounds Cluster* offers a child rhyming games and activities. In this activity cluster he will also find games he will play to learn beginning sound isolation and phoneme segmentation. These lessons that focus on sounds in spoken language are grouped together and displayed prominently on a shelf or tray.

Cluster 1 Alphabet Activities has a variety of games that ask a child to use beginning sound isolation to match picture cards to the letters A - G - H - M - S. Additional letter clusters lead the child sequentially through the rest of the alphabet.

The *3-Letter Word Mastery Cluster* is a collection of activities that guide a student to learn and then practice the decoding process with simple 3-letter short vowel words, like *cat*, *bug* and *hat*. Here the child will use phoneme segmentation to map *all* the sounds of a spoken word onto the correct sequence of letters in a printed word. He will then move on to activity clusters with 4-letter words, 5 & 6-letter words, words with multi-letter combinations (phonograms) and finally to activities with connected text (sentences and books).

As a child is introduced to each new activity cluster, the teacher will demonstrate how one of the games is played, then the child is invited to take a turn. The teacher will take additional turns as needed but will leave the child to work independently when he shows that he understands the activity and is successful with it. Additional games are introduced as the child asks for them or if the teacher needs to guide the child more directly.

The teacher determines when a child has the prerequisite skill or knowledge for an activity cluster, so she only needs to show him how each game is played. Now the child will know where to go to choose his work during a practice session, and over time he will have more and more activities to choose from.

If the skill level of the child matches the games of a cluster, it is a perfect fit. The child finds immediate success and his interest in the self-teaching process is heightened. Add the magical ingredients of choice and repetition, and the alchemy of self-guided learning begins.

When implemented as an intervention program for students who need to pick up dropped stitches and strengthen fundamental literacy skills, these activities are easily learned and mastered. Struggling learners will move through the activity clusters quickly and gain the confidence and mastery they are lacking.

Self-Checking Practice Sheets

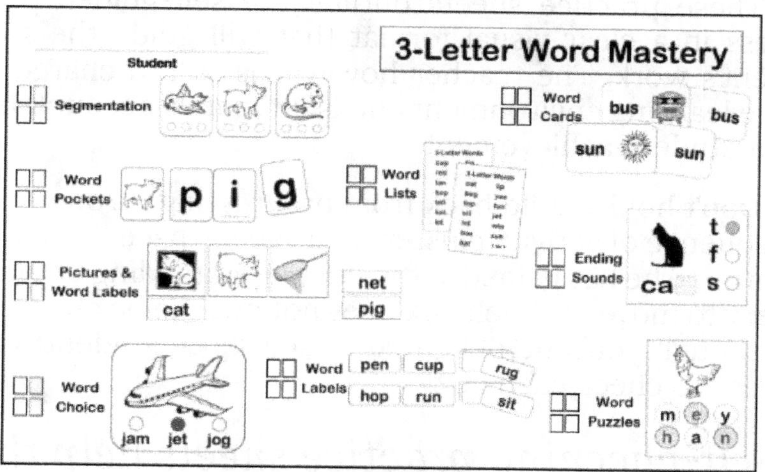

Self-Checking Practice Sheet for 3-Letter Word Reading Mastery

The use of self-checking practice sheets is an important element of this self-guided learning process and helps students share in the responsibility of learning. Each sheet is a different activity cluster with pictures of the various games a student can choose to work with. Next to each game image are little boxes to be checked when he has practiced that activity. A child may not necessarily need to check each box before moving on in the sequence.

Some students are highly motivated by this visual pathway. They love checking off boxes and want to zoom through the sequence. Other students need more encouragement and direction from the teacher, who can use a highlighter to mark the box of an activity she wants the student to practice a bit more.

How you use the self-checking practice sheets will vary depending on the needs and abilities of the individual child. You will undoubtedly find new ways to motivate students and to keep track of their progress.

These practice sheets outline the self-guided process in a clear visual format that will guide the student's work. The teacher however is still in charge of the learning environment and is ultimately accountable for student achievement.

Don't hold a child back from progressing through the sequence of activity clusters at a speedy pace if you determine he has gained sufficient understanding or mastery to move on. Each box does not need to be checked, although you'll be delighted to see those student who want to check each box.

Self-checking practice sheets help the teacher individualize learning for each student.

Likewise, don't let a student move too quickly if you are not seeing sufficient understanding or success. You may need to pencil in extra boxes for the student to check off before he is ready to move on. And all students—particularly the struggling learners who generally need more repetition—are to be encouraged and sometimes directed to practice with activities from previous clusters.

Individualized Instruction

Not every student learns at the same pace. When teaching to a group, you may be teaching quickly, at the pace of your best learners who always excel and who push you to move faster. But you may not always notice when some children are struggling to keep up.

Or you may be moving slowly and deliberately in order to reach your struggling learners, neglecting the advanced learners who are ready to gallop. In both scenarios there are students whose needs for individualized instruction are not being met.

Self-checking practice sheets help the teacher individualize learning for each student.

Even in traditional classrooms, students can have this opportunity to learn at an individual pace with lessons and activities that match their skill level. When learning materials are organized by activity clusters and students are given self-checking practice sheets to guide their choices and track their progress, a lot of work will get done and much learning will happen.

Principles of Effective Early Reading Instruction

From the Concrete to the Abstract, From the Known to the Unknown

This method is based on activities and games that direct the student to move from speech to print, from sound to symbol. Activities that direct the student to move from spoken words (represented by pictures) to printed letters or words strengthen the student's phonemic awareness and alphabet knowledge and reinforce understanding of the alphabetic principle.

This method is based on activities and materials that direct the student to move from speech to print—from sound to symbol.

Additionally, moving from speech to print—from sound to symbol—reflects a basic principle of teaching: always move from the *concrete* to the *abstract*. Begin with something concrete and then associate the abstract concept to that concrete object or sensation.

This guides the child to move from the *known* to the *unknown.*

We don't teach children about math concepts by writing numbers on the chalkboard. We provide colorful beads and blocks for them to count and manipulate. Once a child knows something in the concrete form, we can add abstract symbols or concepts.

Likewise, when introducing our alphabetic system of written language, we want to introduce the concrete first.

Sound *is* concrete. Our body vibrates when we speak a sound or a word. Even when we say a sound silently, our body vibrates.

We begin with the perception of sounds in spoken language, which are concrete. And *then* we introduce abstract symbols that represent those sounds.

With enough repetitions, the concrete and the abstract become interchangeable to the child—fixed in his mind as one thing.

Movement and Hands-On Learning

Movement is key to learning. When movement is involved, the child's brain is stimulated differently than when he is passively watching and listening. Movement directs the mind to deeper understanding.

A child learns best when touching and doing. If we can give the hand something to do, learning happens more easily. A child tends to remember what he can touch or hold in his hand because he is more engaged in his own learning.

Work of the hand focuses the mind and develops concentration. Concentration brings a quiet peacefulness and strengthens the child's memory.

Choice

Effective methods of instruction offer students freedom to choose lessons and activities that interest them. Students are more motivated when they can choose their own activities. This freedom of choice is only limited by where a student is in the learning sequence. It is freedom within a clearly outlined structure and sequence of choices.

Freedom to choose is key to shifting responsibility for learning to the student. It also individualizes the learning experience.

Freedom to choose is key to shifting responsibility for learning to the student. It also individualizes the learning experience for the student, according to his strengths and interests.

One student might be comfortable only working on activities that he already knows and does well. Another student may always be looking for new challenges, loves to choose new activities, and doesn't mind failing at something hard. We want to give students freedom to make the choices that are most comfortable for them and which match their temperament or learning style.

Choice stimulates repetition and interest. Adding a new game to one of the activity clusters is a great way to renew a student's attention and stimulate his interest in learning.

Repetition

Repetition is the healing balm of education. It is the teacher's best teaching tool. Repetition gives a student time to make connections to previously learned skills or information. Repetition helps move a skill from the conscious to the subconscious so that knowledge becomes second nature. That's why games are such effective learning tools. A fun learning game invites repetition which deepens understanding and skill.

Every student requires a different amount of repetition to learn optimally. Students who struggle will often show quick improvement with more repetition.

Students in a self-directed learning environment can get the repetition they need to master important reading skills.

Students in a self-directed learning environment can get the repetition they need to master important reading skills. This repetition may be spontaneous on the part of a student, or it may come at the direction of a teacher who recognizes that a student needs more practice. That is why there are multiple check-off boxes next to each activity on the practice sheets.

Isolation of Difficulty

The activities in this method follow the important principle of isolation of difficulty. This allows a child to focus on—and master—just one skill or piece of knowledge at a time, without the introduction of unnecessary or new information.

These games direct the child to practice and master a skill he has *already* learned. He is not asked to apply a skill he does not yet have or a concept he does not yet understand.

This isolation of difficulty provides more success for a student and creates more motivation.

The isolation of a skill the child has but needs to practice means that the activity or game is not too hard or too easy (or boring!) for him. It rests in that sweet spot that guarantees success, which creates greater motivation to continue.

When the child knows that he will be successful with every activity, he falls into a rhythm of expressing his independence and freedom of choice and makes greater progress in his learning.

As a child progresses in the mastery of basic skills, he can begin to handle multiple elements at the same time and will not be distracted in his learning. Isolating the difficulty is how we help the child build that mastery.

Independence

Independence is a crucial part of this model of self-directed learning and has many benefits.

When a student is not expected to just sit still and listen to the teacher, but can work independently on an activity that matches his interest, he learns better and is more concentrated in his learning. He is not easily distracted.

The teacher can move among students during an independent practice session and quickly recognize and help a struggling learner. She can easily see a child who is ready for a new level of challenge.

Independence allows for differentiation and forms the bedrock of an individualized curriculum.

Students are not expected to all be at the same skill level or to be interested in doing the same activity. Independence allows for differentiation and forms the bedrock of an individualized curriculum. It teaches responsibility and prepares a student for success in school and in life.

In a traditional classroom, freedom to leave the desk to choose a reading game from an activity cluster can be the very thing that ignites the interest and progress of an otherwise reluctant learner.

Order

A structured, well-defined sequence of learning provides a sense of order for beginning readers. It offers them a clear path of success.

Struggling readers often experience a feeling of being lost, of not knowing what they are supposed to do or how to do it. They sense that they are struggling but often don't understand why.

Guided by easy-to-follow practice sheets with activities that are organized by skill, both the beginning and the struggling reader are always clear about which games they can work with and are confident that they will be successful in their work.

An orderly path of learning also guides and supports the teacher, who must keep track of the progress of each student. When students are following a specific sequence of activities and skills, it is much easier for the teacher to see where the individual student is in that sequence and more importantly which students need help and which ones can be encouraged to gallop.

Teaching, Not Testing

Teachers and parents often substitute testing for teaching. A test can give us valuable feedback about what a child knows and what he can do, but it is not an effective teaching technique.

Testing a student on something you *know* he can do is a great way to further anchor that skill, and it is fun for the student who loves to "show what he knows." Testing in that context is a way to reinforce knowledge and skills that are already present in the child.

However, when the student is asked to read a printed letter or word on a page with no prompts from a nearby picture, that is a test! Does the student know the answer? Sadly, many struggling readers don't, which is why they struggle and fail on a daily basis.

Activities with multiple-choice answers are more effective because the correct answer is something the student is already familiar with from previous work.

The independent, self-guided activities in this program reinforce a student's knowledge or skill by providing multiple-choice answers. These little multiple-choice "quizzes" are easy and more effective because the correct answer is something the student is already familiar with from previous work.

The student who is working with this game card has been prepared to succeed from work he has done previously. He has learned to isolate beginning sounds and he has been introduced to the letter H and the sound it makes. The picture of HOUSE is prompting him to find the letter that makes the /h/ sound.

Beginning Sounds & Letters

This game card is a kind of multiple-choice quiz. And because the student immediately recognizes the correct answer, it serves to reinforce the knowledge of that letter-sound.

Beauty

Having an orderly learning environment creates an atmosphere of calm. A calm, well-organized environment is conducive to concentration, exploration and self-directed learning.

An attractive display of learning games and activities is welcoming to young children, particularly struggling learners who need a learning space that is less threatening and more inviting.

Add beauty to your classroom by choosing lesson trays and containers that are colorful and bright. Find interesting and unusual boxes and game pieces that call to the child saying, "Come and play with me."

So many of our young people come from homes and communities that are chaotic and stressful. Create for your students a place of beauty and calm.

How a Child Teaches Himself the Alphabet

Beginning Sound Isolation

The ability to identify the first sound in a spoken word is the foundation for understanding and learning the alphabet. Isolating the beginning sounds of spoken words will guide the child in learning the sounds of the letters A-Z.

The teacher must first teach beginning sound isolation with activities that *model* this isolation skill for the child.

Beginning Sound Bingo Card

Beginning Sound Bingo is one of several games the teacher plays with a student in order to model the "slicing off" of the beginning sound of a word. She'll ask, "Where is /m/..MONKEY?" "Who has /b/.. BALL?"

When a student demonstrates the ability to isolate beginning sounds on his own, we provide activities that allow him to practice this skill with a game like the one below.

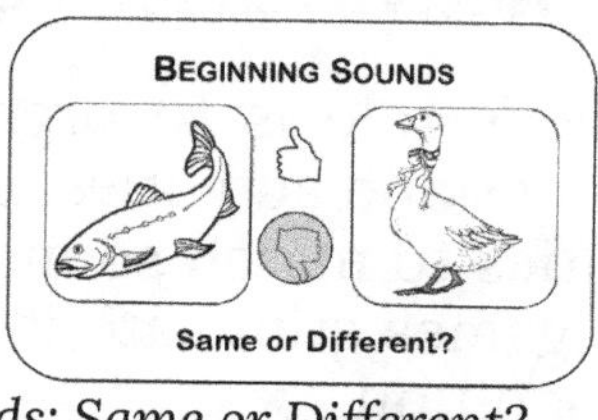

Beginning Sounds: Same or Different?

With practice, beginning sound isolation becomes quick and automatic. The student will use this isolation skill to apply the alphabetic principle and learn the alphabet.

Applying the Alphabetic Principle to Letters

The door to alphabet knowledge is unlocked with beginning sound isolation. When a young child can isolate the beginning sounds of spoken words, he can map those sounds to printed letters and begin the process of teaching himself the letters A-Z.

The Alphabetic Principle at the Letter Level.

This card is an example of the alphabetic principle at the letter level. When the student isolates the beginning sound of LION on this alphabet card, he can map that sound onto the printed letter and read its sound.

The student can now easily identify the sound of any letter that is next to a picture. This is why we teach the alphabetic principle *before* we teach the alphabet.

We teach the alphabetic principle first, then we provide self-guided activities that teach the alphabet.

Games & Activities for Learning the Alphabet

The teacher's role is to organize the self-guided alphabet games and activities, so each student has many opportunities to match sounds to printed letters. Fun, hands-on games stimulate interest and lead to strong letter recognition.

The picture of the MOUSE above is giving the student his marching orders.

Thomas, my beginning sound is /m/. Find the letter that says /m/.

The student uses beginning sound isolation to determine which printed letter matches that beginning sound.

The student is not required to read a letter, just to recognize it when prompted by a sound.

Using the alphabet cards as reference if needed, Thomas will easily recognize and choose the correct letter. This does not require strong letter identification. We are not asking Thomas to *read* the letter "m", just to recognize it when prompted by a sound. This is also a kind of multiple-choice quiz.

Successful recognition of the correct letter makes a very powerful imprint on the child's brain and subconscious mind. He is *seeing* the letter, *saying* the sound of the letter (even if silently) and *hearing* the sound of the letter. Once he learns the game, Thomas can do this matching activity independent of the teacher.

Our goal with beginning learners is to lead them to the application of the alphabetic principle and the recognition of letters by sounds.

The goal for the struggling reader is to strengthen his conscious understanding of the alphabetic principle and to provide easy-to-master alphabet activities organized in a clearly defined sequence that he can move through quickly.

Matching speech sounds to printed letters allows the struggling reader to grasp at a deeper level our alphabetic code and to learn the phonics that he knows only partially but without sufficient automaticity—phonics he may have memorized but which he doesn't fully understand.

Beginning sound isolation forms the foundation of understanding, learning and mastering the alphabet. The goal is automatic letter recognition, which is best achieved by purposeful and fun practice, not by memorization.

How a Child Teaches Himself to Decode

Phoneme Segmentation

The door to decoding words is unlocked with phoneme segmentation. When a child can segment a spoken word into individual sounds, he can map those sounds onto the letters in a printed word and begin the process of teaching himself how to decode.

The ability to break words apart into individual sounds is the foundation for each word-reading activity in this program. Phoneme segmentation will guide him in learning how to decode and spell words.

The teacher must first teach phoneme segmentation with activities that *model* this segmentation skill for the child.

Blending Game Bingo

Blending Game Bingo is one of several games the teacher will play with students that allow her to *model* the segmentation of words into individual sounds. She will ask, "Who has /h/../a/../t/?" "Let's find /b/../u/../g/."

When a student demonstrates the ability to segment a word into sounds on his own, we provide activities that direct him to practice phoneme segmentation so that it becomes quick and automatic. He will use this segmentation skill to learn how to decode words.

Phoneme segmentation forms the foundation of understanding and mastering the decoding process and is therefore the most important reading skill.

Phoneme segmentation forms the foundation of understanding and mastering the decoding process and is therefore the most *important* reading skill. Struggling readers often lack this crucial ability to separate spoken words into individual sounds. Mapping speech sounds onto letters of a printed word strengthens the child's phoneme segmentation skill and creates deeper alphabet knowledge.

Applying the Alphabetic Principle to Words

The student's ability to isolate the three sounds of the word JET allows him to map those sounds onto the nearby letters. This is an example of the alphabetic principle at the word level.

The Alphabetic Principle at the Word Level.

The student can now easily read the letters in a printed word that is next to a picture.

Using his phoneme segmentation skill to apply sounds of *spoken* words to *printed* words, the student starts to teach himself how to decode simple 3 & 4-letter words.

Games & Activities for Learning to Decode

The teacher's role is to organize the self-guided learning games and activities so that each child has many opportunities to map sounds onto printed words and learn to decode.

The child starts with 3-letter highly regular, short vowel words (DOG, PIG, HAT), then moves on to 4-letter words (FLAG, PLUG, CLAP), and later to longer words with 5 and 6 letters (PLANT, STAMP, HELMET).

The teacher will always introduce a new word-reading activity by starting with a picture, *segmenting* that word into individual phonemes and then finding the word with letters that match those sounds.

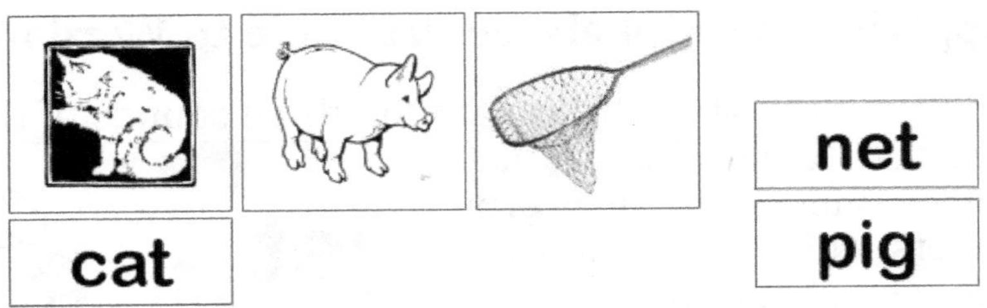

3-Letter Short Vowel Pictures & Labels

The picture of the PIG in this game is giving the student his marching orders.

Veronica, the sounds in my word are /p/../i/../g/.

Find the word that has the letters that match those sounds.

The student uses phoneme segmentation to determine which sequence of printed letters matches that sequence of sounds.

> *Mapping the sounds of a spoken word onto the letters of a printed word sounds exactly like decoding.*

This is not true decoding, but it *mimics* decoding. As the child speaks and maps the spoken sounds onto a printed word, it is an exact *simulation* of the decoding process. It sounds *exactly* like decoding.

Note also that this does not require strong letter identification. The student is not required to read a letter, just to recognize it when prompted by a sound.

In *real* decoding there is no picture to guide the student. He must know the sound of each letter of a word so he can blend them together to identify the word. In *real* decoding he starts with the unknown and must discover a word he knows. Decoding the 3-letter word SUN is a *test* with 3 questions he must answer. This requires accurate (i.e. strong) letter identification which is always a stumbling block for struggling readers.

Practice materials with pictures that depict spoken words will help a struggling reader who can already decode, but not very well. Moving from speech to print and mapping sounds of a spoken word to letters of a printed word allows him to grasp at a deeper level what decoding is—what it sounds and feels like to decode. This strengthens his decoding, which starts to become more fluent and automatic.

This mapping process will also strengthen his letter recognition and phoneme segmentation skills and offer the many successful repetitions needed to make simple one-syllable decodable words into *sight words*—words that are read automatically, without the need to sound out each letter. With successful decoding practice, the student subconsciously begins to learn how to read words automatically, an ability that grows stronger over time.

Organizing the Self-Directed Learning Environment

The organization of materials in the environment is crucial to early reading success. The games and activities for each skill level should be grouped together in an attractive manner and made easily accessible to the student.

These activity clusters give students a clear awareness of where they are in the learning sequence and which activities are available to them for practice in a self-directed learning environment.

This learning sequence is not a sequence of individual lessons or games that the teacher must lead a child through. Rather it is a sequence of activity clusters, each offering the child multiple games to choose from.

The only check on this freedom of choice is the teacher, who determines whether a student is ready for a particular activity cluster and who at times will assign an activity to the student. She may do this to be sure his practice session is productive and on-target, and that he is getting sufficient repetition.

The self-checking practice sheets illustrate games that can be included in an activity cluster. Any activities that the students like to play and which the teacher finds useful can be included in an activity cluster.

However, the majority of the games in a cluster need to have pictures that will prompt students with sounds they can match to letters and words. The option to move from *sound* to *symbol* is crucial to effective early reading instruction and intervention programs.

Supervised Practice

This model of reading instruction consists primarily of supervised practice, not direct teaching. Learning is achieved through the child's own independent practice. It is through the student's practice of materials that match his skill level that he achieves mastery of those skills. The emphasis on independent learning creates a shift in the learning environment from a traditional model of memorization through drill, to a deeper, more permanent learning that comes through meaningful self-guided practice.

The teacher's most important role is that of observing the success and struggles of individual students during practice sessions.

Did a student complete the work quickly or slowly? Or somewhere in between?

Do mistakes show a pattern of confusion or of guessing? Or are those mistakes merely a product of disinterest or distracted attention?

Is that student ready to move on to the next cluster?

These are the questions you will be asking yourself as you walk about during practice sessions, looking on at the work being done. The practice sheets help you individualize the learning and track the progress for each student.

Self-checking practice sheets help the teacher individualize learning for each student.

In a supervised practice session, reading progress is best achieved when a student begins to take on responsibility for his own learning. The teacher is ultimately accountable, however, to see that the student is successful and that progress is achieved.

When a student can isolate beginning sounds, he has the key to enter the door marked *LETTERS*. There he will learn games and activities to gain strong alphabet knowledge.

The struggling reader can move through the alphabet clusters quickly. He already has the beginning sound isolation skill and an (unsteady) ability to read letters. He just needs to gain a stronger grasp of how sounds and letters match, and a greater mastery of letter knowledge.

The self-checking practice sheets will guide his practice, and the teacher will supervise practice sessions in a joyful, encouraging manner. This struggling reader will shore up his alphabet knowledge and learn to take responsibility for his learning.

When a student has *phoneme segmentation*, he has the key to enter the door marked WORDS. There he will learn games and activities that ask him to apply this segmentation skill to learn how to decode. We've seen earlier how this mapping process mimics the actual decoding process.

The child will have a variety of games that teach him to decode and that continue to strengthen his phoneme segmentation and letter recognition. The self-checking practice sheets will guide his practice, and the teacher will supervise the practice sessions in a joyful, encouraging manner.

In a self-directed learning environment, students have a choice of games within an appropriate activity cluster. They are given freedom to move and to choose and repeat activities they are successful with. This is freedom within the limits of a clearly organized structure.

The student understands that he has work to do and he understands what games are available to him. The work is fun because success is fun. Self-confidence blossoms. The love of learning grows.

Intervention for Struggling Readers

Struggling readers already have some alphabet knowledge and decoding skills. They usually have a significant level of phonemic awareness. But their foundational reading skills are not solid enough for them to keep up with their classmates and feel good about themselves.

Rapid progress for struggling readers is joyful and extremely empowering. Self-confidence blossoms.

The reading resource teacher or tutor will find great benefit from organizing the learning environment in activity clusters, implementing the use of self-checking practice sheets, and redefining her role in the classroom. Struggling readers will begin to experience rapid success, which is joyful and extremely empowering for them. The teacher herself will find that she is able to give more focused help to those who need it. She will have more time to notice which students need to spend more time at a specific skill level and which students are ready to move on in the sequence.

Now, instead of giving direct instruction to individuals or to small groups of students, the resource teacher is supervising joyful and productive practice sessions. She moves from student to student, quickly checking their work, making mental notes of their progress and stopping only to give aid or encouragement to her hard-working students.

Part II
Implementing the Method

Overview

The sequence of activities that follows gives beginning and struggling readers a concrete understanding of the alphabetic principle, strong letter knowledge, confident decoding and fluent word identification.

Each activity is included on self-checking practice sheets (See Appendix C) that students will use during independent practice sessions. The teacher may include other phonemic awareness activities she has found to be interesting and useful to her students.

Phonemic Awareness

Printed letters represent sounds, and the student's ability to isolate sounds in spoken words—called phonemic awareness—is essential to learning to read in our alphabetic writing system. The ability to hear and manipulate the sounds in spoken language is a strong predictor of early reading success.

In this program the student's ability to isolate the beginning sounds of spoken words will guide him in learning the sounds of the letters A-Z.

Each activity in this section is included on self-checking practice sheets which students will use during independent practice sessions. The teacher may include other phonemic awareness activities she has found to be interesting and useful to her students.

Note: The ability to rhyme is not a strong predictor of later reading achievement, but including rhyming activities is a playful way for a young child to explore spoken language. (See Appendix D for rhyming games and activities.)

Beginning Sound Isolation

Beginning Sound Bingo
Item #111

Purpose:

- To model isolation of the beginning sounds of spoken words
- To prepare the student to understand the alphabetic principle—that letters represent sounds
- To prepare the student to learn the sounds of the letters A-Z

Activity:

1. Give the student a Beginning Sound Bingo Card.
2. Call out a picture you see on the student's card, isolating the beginning sound as you say the word.

   /mmm/..MONKEY.

3. The student places a game piece on the picture of MONKEY and repeats,

   /mmm/..MONKEY.

4. Continue calling out pictures you see on the student's card in this same manner.

   /b/..BALLOONS.
   /b/..BALL.

5. When the student fills up his game card, ask him to choose another card and continue the game.

6. Show the student the image for this activity on the Activities with Sounds self-checking practice sheet. He may ask a teacher to play this game with him during practice sessions.

Supplemental activities:

1. Call a student by saying his name with the beginning sound.

   */d/..*DAVE *is ready.*
   */sss/..*SALLY *may line up for lunch.*

2. Ask a student to tell you what he sees out the window or while on a walk. When the student spots a dog say,

   */d/..*DOG. *What else do you see?*

3. Randomly slice off the beginning sound of a word.

   *Karen, please bring me that /p/..*PENCIL.

Notes:

- When a young child can isolate the beginning sounds of spoken words, you can show him how to map those sounds onto letters and he can begin the process of teaching himself the sound each letter makes.

- When isolating the beginning sounds of words that have a hard consonant sound, keep the phoneme crisp and discrete. Do not add a vowel sound ('uh") at the end of the phoneme. Do not say, "/duh/.. DOG."
- In addition to modeling beginning sound isolation, this bingo activity teaches the vocabulary of the pictures on the cards. Later the student will use these bingo cards to practice beginning sound isolation independently.
- The student's own voice is more important to his brain than your voice. Encourage the student to repeat the "beginning sound stories" he hears from you (e.g. /b/..BALL) as he places his game piece. This should quickly become part of the game rules.
- Because a student verbally repeats a beginning sound, it doesn't mean he can isolate beginning sounds on his own. Don't ask a student to identify the beginning sound of a word until you are confident that he can do it. For now, he is just repeating what he hears you say.
- Activities for teaching blending should be done parallel to work with beginning sound isolation, though ideally not in the same learning session.

Beginning Sound Cards: Independent Practice Item #111

Prerequisite skill: The student can isolate beginning sounds.

Purpose:

- Practice isolating the beginning sounds of spoken words
- Preparation for learning the sounds of the letters of the alphabet

Activity:

1. Choose a Beginning Sound Card and show the student how to work with it independently.

   We start here in the box at the top.
   *I'll put a game piece on the /b/..*BALL.
   Let's find all the pictures on the card that start with /b/.

2. Isolate the beginning sound of each picture and place a game piece on those images with the same beginning sound as the key picture.
3. Invite the student to choose a card and take a turn.
4. Alternate turns as needed to help the student understand the game concept and work independently.
5. Show the student the image for this activity on the Activities with Sounds self-checking practice sheet. He may now choose to play this game during practice sessions.

Notes:

- When a child can successfully and consistently isolate beginning sounds, introduce the alphabetic principle and begin work with letters.

- Activities for teaching blending should be done parallel to work with beginning sound isolation.

Beginning Sounds: Same or Different?
Item #112

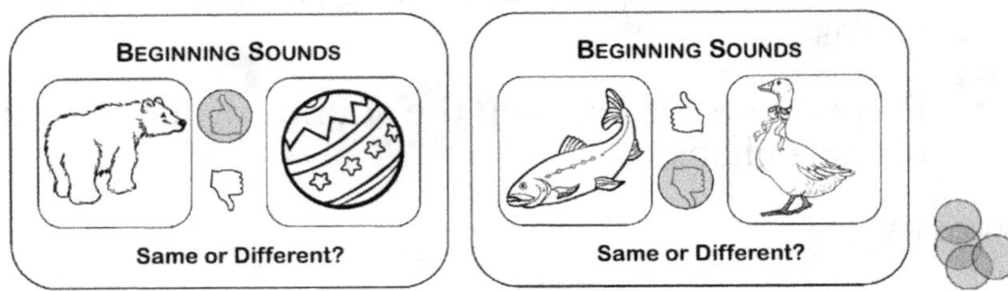

Prerequisite skill: The student can isolate beginning sounds.

Purpose:

- Practice isolating the beginning sounds of spoken words
- Preparation for learning the sounds of the letters of the alphabet

Activity:

1. Choose a Same or Different? card.
2. Identify the vocabulary of the two pictures on the card.

   BEAR. BALL.

3. Isolate the beginning sounds to determine if they are the "same or different."

   */b/..*BEAR. */b/..*BALL.
   BEAR *and* BALL *both start with /b/.*
   I'll put a game piece on 'thumbs up'.

4. Choose another Same or Different? card and take another turn. Be sure to give the vocabulary and isolate the beginning sound of each picture before determining if they are "same or different."
5. Invite the student to have a turn and alternate turns as needed to help the student understand the game concept and work independently.
6. Show the student the image for this activity on the Activities with Sounds self-checking practice sheet. He may now choose to play this game during practice sessions.

Notes:

- Once a child can successfully and consistently isolate beginning sounds, he can be introduced to the alphabetic principle and begin his work with letters.
- Activities for teaching blending should be done parallel to work with beginning sound isolation.

Blending

The blending activities below should be introduced along with beginning sound activities, though ideally not in the same learning session.

Blending is a skill a student will need when he begins to decode. After "sounding out" the letters in a word (/c/../a/../t/), the student must *blend* the sounds together to identify the word (CAT).

Blending games allow the teacher to model *phoneme segmentation* for her students.

The Blending Game
Item #120

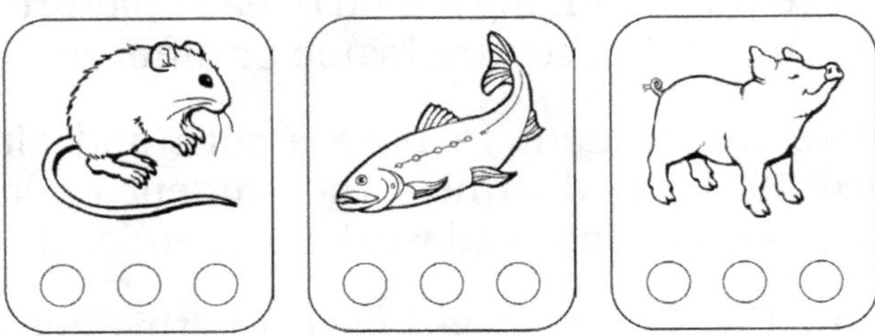

Purpose:

- To blend sounds into words in preparation for learning to decode
- To model phoneme segmentation for the student
- To prepare the student to understand the alphabetic principle at the word level
- To prepare the student to encode and decode 3 letter words

Activity:

1. Place two picture cards on the workspace in front of the student, naming the vocabulary as you do so.

   MOUSE.
   FISH.

2. Ask the student to find one of the cards by segmenting the word into sounds instead of saying the word normally.

   Where is the /m/../ow/../s/?

3. When the student chooses the correct picture card, ask him to say the word. Cards he guesses correctly are placed in a stack nearby.

4. Replace that picture card with another and ask him to choose another card.

   Where is the /p/../i/../g/?

5. The student needs to say the word before he picks up the card and places it in his stack.

6. Once the student has collected a stack of five or six picture cards, take the stack and hold it close to you with the pictures facing away from the child. Ask the student to guess what picture you are hiding. As before, you will segment the word into sounds instead of saying it normally.

   What picture am I hiding?
   /f/../i/../sh/.

7. When the student guesses the word correctly, give him the card and continue working through the cards from his stack.

8. If the student guesses wrong, show him the card, say the correct word and then put that card at the back of your stack.

9. When you are confident that the student understands the game concept, continue playing the Blending Game in this same manner using the full deck of picture cards.

10. If hiding the cards is still too difficult or in any way confusing for the student, go back to the first technique of placing two or more cards in front of the student so he can see the pictures before he chooses.

11. Show the student the image for this activity on the Activities with Sounds self-checking practice sheet. He may now ask a teacher to play this game with him during practice sessions.

Challenge Activity:

1. To increase the challenge of the Blending Game, separate the sounds a bit further apart (*/f/..../i/..../sh/*).
2. Continue to separate the phonemes further and further (/f/....../i/....../sh/) as appropriate to keep the game challenging but not too hard. If the student answers incorrectly, you have separated the phonemes too far. Simply segment the word again and bring the phonemes a bit closer together.
3. You are playing the game correctly if the student always gives the right answer, but the game isn't too easy for him and therefore uninteresting.

Notes:

- You can individualize The Blending Game for each student when playing with a group. For one student you might place two or more picture cards on the table for him to choose from. For another student you might hide the pictures and segment the words with the sounds spoken closely together. With another student you might give the sounds with increasingly greater separation.
- This game gives a student excellent blending skill that he will use when he begins to decode words.
- The Blending Game mimics what it will sound like to the student when he decodes a word and must "sound out" the letters and then blend them to identify the word.

- Each time you give the student sounds to blend, you are modeling for him the breaking apart of spoken words into individual phonemes. He will thus learn this phoneme segmentation skill and then use it later to spell (encode) and read (decode) words.

- When the student is able to segment words on his own, he can play the role of teacher. He will hide a picture card and give 3 sounds that you or other students blend to guess the picture.

- When appropriate for an individual student, introduce The Blending Game Set 2 cards that have 4 phonemes and are more challenging.

- Working with words that have 4 phonemes prepares a student to read and spell 4-letter short vowel words, like FLAT, DUST and STOP.

Blending Game Bingo
Item #114

Purpose:

- To blend sounds into words in preparation for learning to decode

- To model phoneme segmentation for the student

- To prepare the student to understand the alphabetic principle at the word level
- To prepare the student to encode and decode 3 letter words

Activity:

1. Give the student a Blending Game Bingo card.
2. Call out a picture you see on the student's card by segmenting the word into sounds.

   Where is /c/../a/../t/?

3. The student will place a game piece on the picture of CAT and say "cat."
4. Continue calling out pictures on the student's card by segmenting the words into phonemes.

   Find the /b/../u/../g/?
   Where is /sh/../ar/../k/?
   /h/../a/../t/.

5. When the student fills up his game card, he can choose another card and continue the game.
6. Show the student the picture for this activity on the Activities with Sounds self-checking practice sheet. He may now ask a teacher to play this game with him during practice sessions.

Notes:

- The Blending Bingo Game teaches the student how to blend sounds into a word he knows. Later when he is decoding, he will sound out letters and blend them into words.
- Each time you give the student sounds to blend, you are modeling for him the breaking apart of

spoken words into individual phonemes. He will thus learn this phoneme segmentation skill and then later use it to spell (encode) and read (decode) words.

- Don't ask a student to segment a word unless you are relatively sure he is ready to do so.
- Later, when he is able to segment words, the student can play the role of teacher (or "bingo caller").
- The Blending Game activities should be done parallel to work with beginning sound isolation.
- When appropriate for an individual student, introduce The Blending Game Bingo cards that have 4 phonemes and are more challenging.
- Working with words that have 4 phonemes prepares a student to read and spell 4-letter short vowel words like FLAT, DUST and STOP.

Blending Games with 4 Phonemes
Items #121, 114

Activity:

1. When a student can successfully blend three (3) phonemes that have been separated quite far apart (e.g. "/sh/......../ar/......../k/--SHARK!"), introduce blending games that have 4 phonemes.

2. Begin by keeping the 4 phonemes close together so the student can become familiar with the new vocabulary words in the set. Then, as done previously, begin to separate the sounds further and further apart as appropriate.

Phoneme Segmentation

Phoneme segmentation is an important predictor of reading and spelling ability and guides the child as he learns to decode. Struggling readers often lack this ability to separate spoken words into individual sounds.

Teacher-Guided Phoneme Segmentation
Item #120

Prerequisite Skill: The student is very good at phoneme blending.

Purpose: To guide a student into independent phoneme segmentation

Activity:

1. Take one of the cards from The Blending Game Set 1 [3 sounds].
2. As you segment the word into phonemes, move your finger into the circles beneath the picture, from left-to-right.
3. Ask the student to segment the *same* picture and to move his fingers into the three circles left-to-right as he says the sounds.
4. Continue in this same manner with three or four more cards. Make a small stack of the picture cards that you and the student have segmented together.
5. Take a card from this stack and ask the student to say the sounds of that word as he moves his fingers into the circles, left to right.
6. If the student is relatively successful, have him continue with more cards from this stack. If he is unable to segment the pictures, you may need to go back to the previous step where you segment words with your finger moving into the circles and then ask the student to segment the *same* picture in the same manner.
7. When appropriate ask the child to segment words with picture cards that you have not worked on together.

Notes:

- A student's first attempts at phoneme segmentation are often not very precise. That's OK. This is just a first activity designed to ease a student into segmentation—something he has heard you do many times.

- There is no need to correct a student when his segmentation is not precise and he is not giving discrete, individual phonemes. Perhaps he is not separating the sounds completely, for example "/**ba**/../g/" or "/c/../**up**/".
- You may need to model segmentation—in the above manner with your finger—on several more occasions until he is more successful.

The Blending Game: The Student is the Teacher

Prerequisite Skill: The student can segment words with 3 phonemes

Purpose: Independent phoneme segmentation practice

Activity:

1. Ask the student to be the teacher, using cards from The Blending Game Set 1 or the cards from Beginning Sound Bingo.
2. The student will segment words and ask you to "guess" the picture or to place a game piece on the correct picture.

Note: If the student segments the word poorly, rather than correct him simply repeat the three sounds in a crisp, distinct manner as you *pretend* to think about what the answer could be. Then give the answer. In other words, model the correct segmentation of the word for the student before "guessing" the picture correctly.

The Faye Game

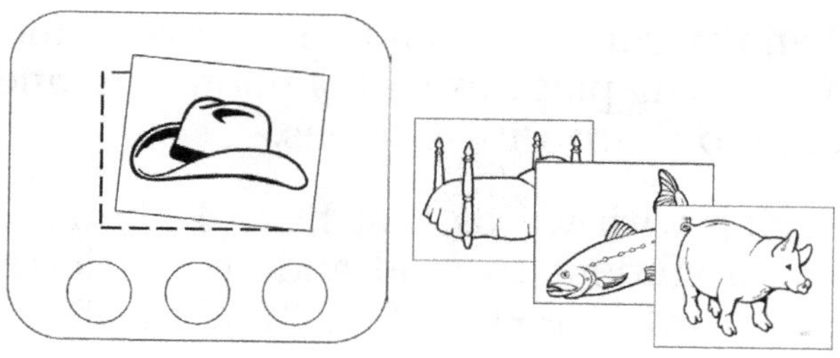

Prerequisite Skill: The student can segment words with 3 phonemes

Purpose: Independent phoneme segmentation practice

Materials:

- Picture cards of words containing only 3 phonemes
- A segmentation card with 3 circles

Activity:

1. Place the stack of cards on the workspace with pictures face down.
2. Place a picture card on the segmentation card above the circles.
3. Segment the word as you move your finger into the circles from left to right.
4. Pace the card into a *discard* stack.
5. Invite the student to take a turn and alternate turns as needed until he can work independently.

Notes:

- When the student is ready, The Faye Game can be played using pictures with 4 phonemes and a segmentation card with 4 circles.
- Working with words that have 4 phonemes prepares a student to read and spell 4-letter short vowel words like FLAT, DUST and STOP.

Teaching the Alphabet

The organizing principle of the learning environment is the display of games and activities that are grouped according to *skill*.

The self-directed alphabet work is divided into 5 activity clusters, each containing games for learning a group of 5 letters. You may choose to create different letter groupings, but the principle of organizing the letters by clusters is essential—for the student and for the teacher.

The activities are included on the self-checking practice sheets that students will use during independent practice sessions. The teacher may include other activities in these clusters that she has found to be interesting and useful to her students, but they must be organized according to the letter clusters.

The student benefits from this cluster sequence because it gives him a clear roadmap to reading success, and he will get the fun repetition needed for alphabet mastery. Seeing the path so clearly laid out can be very motivating to a student. As he moves through the clusters, he gains a strong sense of success. This sense of success is often lacking in struggling readers.

A struggling reader who needs to strengthen his alphabet mastery will easily understand the games in these alphabet clusters and can work independently right away.

The speed and accuracy with which a student completes cluster #1 alphabet activities will indicate his readiness to move to the next cluster. Alphabet mastery is a function of *accuracy* and *speed.*

The Alphabetic Principle

The student will use beginning sound isolation to connect the sounds of spoken language to printed letters and begin to identify and learn the alphabet. This relationship between sounds and letters—the *alphabetic principle*—will be his guide as he learns to read and spell.

Alphabet Cards
Item #200 (Small)

Prerequisite skill: The student can isolate beginning sounds.

Purpose: To show the student how to use beginning sound isolation to identify the sound of a letter that is next to a key picture

Materials: Alphabet Cards for cluster #1 letters A-G-H-M-S

Activity:

1. Introduce the Cluster #1 alphabet cards by naming each picture, isolating the beginning sound and

then pointing to the letter and saying the sound again.

> APPLE.
> /a/..APPLE.
> *This letter says /a/.*
>
> GOAT.
> /g/..GOAT.
> *This letter says /g/.*

2. Go through the set of five cards again, letting the student tell *you* the sound of each letter by isolating the beginning sound of the picture.

Notes:

- The alphabetic principle should be introduced as soon as a student is able to isolate beginning sounds of spoken words.
- A student who can identify the sound of a letter that is next to a key picture doesn't necessarily "know" that letter. It doesn't mean he will remember the sound of that letter yet. But this shows that the student can apply the *alphabetic principle* and understands how to map sounds to letters.

Alphabet Activities

Letter & Picture Sorting
Item #200 (S), Item #211

Prerequisite skills:

- The student can isolate beginning sounds of spoken words.
- The student has been introduced to the alphabet cards and can identify the sound of a letter that is next to a key picture.

Materials:

- Alphabet Cards for cluster #1 letters A-G-H-M-S
- Letter & Picture Sorting cards for cluster #1 letters A-G-H-M-S

Purpose:

- To match the beginning sounds of spoken words to printed letters
- To gain strong recognition of the cluster #1 letters

Activity:

1. Place the cluster #1 alphabet cards in a row at the top of the workspace, pictures facing up.
2. As a review, ask the student to identify the sounds of the letters on the alphabet cards.

3. Place the deck of picture cards face down.

4. Take a card, identify the picture, isolate its beginning sound, and place the card beneath the letter that matches that beginning sound. Be sure to make it clear to the child that you are using the key picture as a guide to help you find the correct letter.

   MONKEY.
   /mmm/..MONKEY.

   There's the letter /m/ next to the picture of /m/..MOON.
   So the picture of MONKEY *goes there.*

5. Take another turn in order to model the process again.

6. Invite the student to have a turn and then alternate turns as needed until the student can work independently. Independence with this lesson may not happen with this first presentation.

7. Show the student the image for this activity on the Cluster #1 Alphabet Activities self-checking practice sheet. He may now choose to play this game during practice sessions.

Challenge Activity:

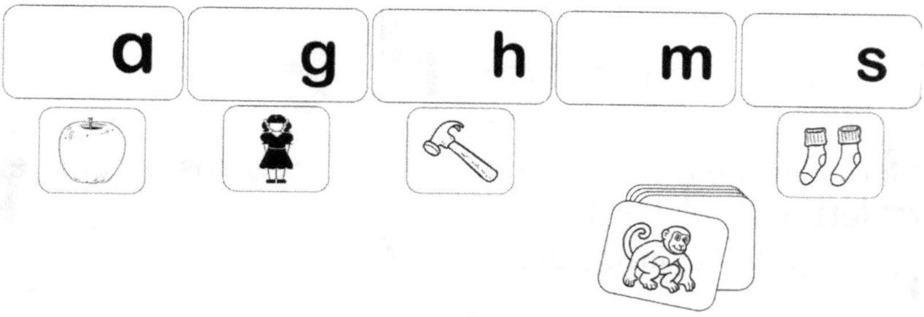

1. When the student is confident in sorting the pictures, introduce a challenge by turning the Alphabet Cards so the key pictures are face down.
2. Ask the student to sort the picture cards without help from the key pictures.

Notes:

- You may need to work with a young child several times on this challenge activity before he is successful working independently with it.
- This is a kind of multiple-choice quiz. The student is not asked to read a letter, only to *recognize* it when prompted by the beginning sound of a picture card he chooses.
- Show the student the image for this activity on the Cluster #1 Alphabet Activities self-checking practice sheet. He may now choose to play this game during practice sessions.

Beginning Sounds & Letters
Item #210

Materials: Beginning Sounds & Letters cards for cluster #1 letters A-G-H-M-S

Prerequisite skills:

- The student can isolate the beginning sounds of spoken words.

- The student is familiar with Cluster #1 letters A-G-H-M-S.

Purpose:

- To practice matching beginning sounds to printed letters
- To gain stronger recognition of the cluster #1 letters

Activity:

1. Place the deck of Beginning Sounds & Letters cards face down.
2. Take a card from the deck, identify the picture and isolate its beginning sound.

   This is a MONKEY. */mmm/*..MONKEY.

3. Say /m/ as you place a game piece on the letter "m."
4. Carefully slide the card to the top of the workspace to begin forming an orderly display of the completed work.
5. Take another turn in order to model the process again.
6. Invite the student to have a turn and alternate turns as needed until he can work independently.
7. Show the student the image for this activity on the Cluster #1 Alphabet Activities self-checking

practice sheet. He may now choose to play this game during practice sessions.

Notes:

- *Do not* read the three letters on the card in order to find the answer. We are not asking the student to read the letters, only to *recognize* the correct letter when prompted by a beginning sound.
- This is a kind of multiple-choice quiz. Eventually the child is asked to decode words without picture clues, which will be a *test* of his ability to read letters.

Letter & Picture Match
Item #218

Prerequisite skill: The student can recognize cluster #1 letters when prompted by a beginning sound.

Materials: Letter & Picture Match cards for cluster #1 letters A-G-H-M-S

Purpose:

- To practice matching beginning sounds to printed letters
- To gain stronger recognition of the cluster #1 letters

Activity:

1. Place the deck of Letter & Picture Match cards face down.

2. Take a card from the deck and identify the beginning sound of each picture on the card to see if it matches the letter. If it matches, it gets a game piece.

   SEAL *starts with /s/.*
   That letter is not a /s/.

   GIRL *starts with /g/.*
   That letter is a /g/.
   I'll put a game piece on GIRL.

3. Continue in the same manner until game pieces have been placed on the appropriate pictures.

4. Carefully slide the completed card near the top of the workspace to begin forming an orderly display of the completed work.

5. Take another turn in order to model the process again.

6. Invite the student to have a turn and alternate additional turns as needed until he can work independently.

7. Show the student the image for this activity on the Cluster #1 Alphabet Activities self-checking practice sheet. He may now choose to play this game during practice sessions.

Notes:

- It is important that the teacher demonstrate this game by beginning with the picture and then seeing if the sound matches the letter. Always move from speech to print, from sound to symbol.
- The student is not asked to read the letter, only to *recognize* it when prompted by the beginning sound of a picture.

Assessing Alphabet Mastery

Materials: Alphabet Cards for cluster #1 letters A-G-H-M-S

Prerequisite: The student has successfully worked with the cluster #1 letter activities.

Activity:

1. Place the cluster #1 Alphabet Key Cards face down so the key pictures are hidden. (As an alternative you may use the image on the Cluster #1 Alphabet Activities self-checking practice sheet.)
2. Ask the student to touch or point to letters you call out at random.

   Where is the /m/?
   Show me the /g/.
   Point to the /a/.
3. Move the cards into a different order and repeat.

4. If the student shows he is successful choosing the letters correctly, move the cards into a different order again and then ask, “Show me the letters you know.” This will give you another good indication of the student’s knowledge of these five letter-sounds without making it seem like a test.

Note: If the student shows strong *recognition*, he should move on to the alphabet activities for cluster #2 letters. He does not need to *read* the cluster #1 letters perfectly.

Sequence of Alphabet Clusters

Alphabet Cluster #1

Alphabet Cluster #2

Alphabet Cluster #3

Alphabet Cluster #4

Alphabet Cluster #5

The X alphabet card may be used to teach the pronunciation of the /ks/ sound made by the letter X at the end of words.

Prerequisite skill:

- The student has good recognition of cluster #1 letters.
- The student can work independently with each cluster #1 activity.

Purpose: To learn the sounds of the alphabet letters A-Z in an orderly sequence.

Materials:

- Alphabet Cards divided into clusters

- Letter & Picture Sorting cards divided into clusters
- Beginning Sounds & Letters cards divided into clusters
- Letter & Picture Match cards divided into clusters
- Other interesting alphabet activities divided into clusters

Notes:

- The student has worked with each of the cluster #1 alphabet activities. As he moves into each new cluster in the sequence, he can be expected to do these activities independently.
- Key to a student's success is how you prepare the learning environment. The various games and activities for each cluster should be grouped together in an attractive manner and easily accessible by the student.
- The student may choose any of the activities in an alphabet cluster in any sequence he desires. He doesn't have to work with each game—some activities are more interesting to a student than others—but he does need to show solid recognition of the letters in a cluster before moving to the next.
- Ongoing evaluation of letter recognition is important.

3-Letter Word Activities

The following 3-letter short vowel word activities are to be displayed together on one shelf or tray. Images of these activities are on the self-checking practice sheets that students will use during independent practice sessions.

The teacher may include other 3-letter word activities she has found to be interesting and useful to her students.

The student is ready to work with words when he is able to segment words with three phonemes, like PIG, DOG and SUN.

The student is not asked to read letters in the word games below; he is asked only to identify or recognize letters prompted by the sounds in the word he is segmenting. This level of letter recognition is quite easy at this point.

Activities in this word activity cluster teach a student how to decode but do not *require* him to decode. The pictures in each game prompt the student to match sounds to letters.

The matching of sounds to letters in words sounds exactly like decoding, and so the student is learning how to decode while not actually being asked to decode.

The teacher will introduce the student to each of the games in the 3-Letter Word Cluster, but word-building activities are a good place to start because encoding words is the most powerful way to teach decoding.

When he is ready to move on in the sequence of word clusters, he will already be familiar with the activities he finds there and can work independently.

3-Letter Word Pockets
Item #300

Prerequisite:

- The student can segment spoken words with 3 phonemes.
- The student has good recognition of the letters A to Z.

Purpose: Preparation for decoding 3-letter short vowel words

Activity:

1. Choose a word pocket. Remove the cards and place them neatly in a random order.
2. Identify the picture and segment the word into 3 phonemes.

   PIG. */p/../i/../g/.*

3. As you segment the word a second time, move the letter cards into the correct position left to right to build the word.
4. Move the letter cards back into a random order and ask the student to build *the same* word.
5. Invite the student to choose a word pocket and build a word.
6. Alternate turns as needed until he can work independently.

Notes:

- Encoding is the most powerful way to teach decoding.
- This "spelling" activity *is* reading instruction. It is reading instruction the student is giving himself, independent of the teacher.

3-Letter Word Puzzles
Item #340

Prerequisite:

- The student can segment spoken words with 3 phonemes.

- The student has good recognition of the letters A to Z.

Purpose:

- To match the sounds of a spoken word to printed letters
- Phoneme segmentation practice
- Direct preparation for decoding

Activity:

1. Take a card from the stack that is placed face-down.
2. Identify the picture and segment the word into 3 phonemes.

   HEN. */h/../e/../n/.*

3. As you segment the word again, place transparent game pieces on the corresponding letters left to right.
4. Invite the student to take a turn and alternate turns as needed.

3-Letter Word Cards
Item #310

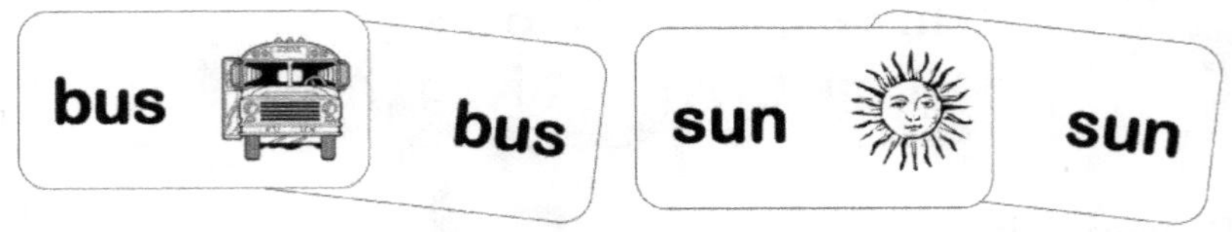

Prerequisites:

- The student can segment spoken words with 3 phonemes.

- The student has good recognition of the letters A to Z.

Purpose:

- To introduce decoding
- Phoneme segmentation practice
- Direct preparation for decoding without picture clues

Activity #1:

1. Take a card from the stack that is placed face-down.
2. Identify the picture and segment the word into 3 phonemes.

   BUS. */b/../u/../s/.*

3. As you segment the word again, move your finger beneath the three letters from left to right. Then say the word as you touch the picture. You can say,

   I am reading with my finger.

4. Invite the student to read the same card in the same manner.
5. Take another turn in order to model the process again.
6. Alternate turns with the student as needed until the student can "read with his finger" as you have demonstrated to him.

Notes:

- The student is using phoneme segmentation to read the letters correctly.
- This activity mimics what actual decoding looks like, sounds like and feels like.

Activity #2:

1. The student holds the deck of cards near his chest so you can't see the pictures.
2. He "decodes" the word in the manner he has been shown and you guess the hidden picture.

Challenge Activity:

1. Place the stack of word cards face down.
2. Decode the word on the top card then flip it over to see if you are right.
3. If you are right, the card is added to your personal stack. If you are incorrect, the card goes to the bottom of the stack.
4. Take another turn and then invite the student to take a turn.
5. Alternate turns as necessary until the student understands how to play the game.

Notes:

- Because the pictures are face down, the child is being asked to decode a word without any picture clue. He will get some right and he will get some wrong, but he has been well-prepared to tackle this decoding challenge. As he goes through this set multiple times, he gains greater accuracy and speed in reading letters and blending them quickly into the correct word.

- This is a perfect activity for a small group of students to play together.

3-Letter Pictures & Word Labels
Item #320

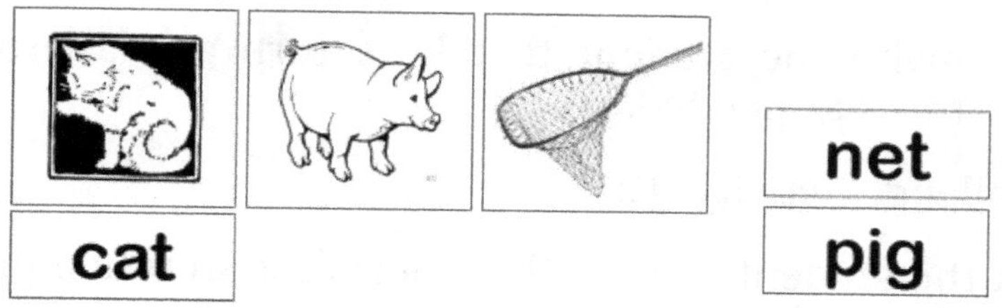

Prerequisites:

- The student can segment spoken words with 3 phonemes.
- The student has good recognition of the letters A to Z.

Purpose: Decoding practice

Activity:

1. Place the picture cards in a row left-to-right, giving the vocabulary of the pictures as you go.
2. Place the word labels in a column to the right of the picture cards.
3. Point to the first picture card, say the word and segment the sounds.

   CAT. */c/../a/../t/.*

4. Search for the CAT label. Check that the letters on the label match the segmented sounds, then place the label beneath the picture.
5. Take another turn so the student clearly sees how you are playing the game—that you are starting with a picture card, then finding the letters that match the sounds of that word.
6. Invite the student to take a turn and alternate turns as needed.

Challenge Activity #1:

Ask the student to read the labels first and then place them beneath the correct picture.

Challenge Activity #2:

After the labels have been placed correctly, turn the picture cards face down and ask the student to read the labels without seeing the pictures. Turn over the picture cards to check your work as you go.

Note: This material should be divided into smaller sets of approximately 10 pictures and 10 labels. Otherwise there are too many individual pieces to keep the materials neatly organized on the workspace.

3-Letter Word Choice Game
Item #330

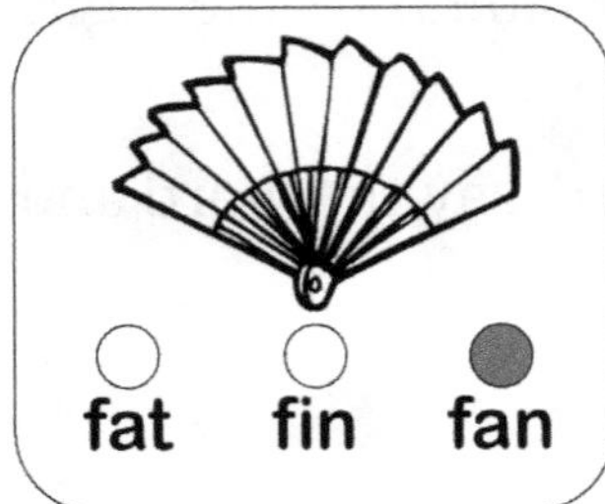

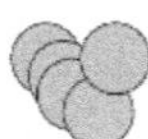

Activity:

1. Take a card from the stack that is placed face-down.
2. Identify the picture and segment the sounds.

   FAN. */f/../a/../n/.*

3. Search for the word that says FAN, matching sounds to letters, starting with the word on the left, until you find the correct word.
4. Place the game piece in the circle above the answer.
5. Take another turn so the student clearly sees how you are playing the game—that you are starting with the picture, then finding the letters that match the sounds of that word.
6. Carefully slide the card to the top of the workspace to begin forming an orderly display of the completed work.
7. Invite the student to take a turn and take additional turns as needed.

3-Letter Action Word Labels & Environment Labels

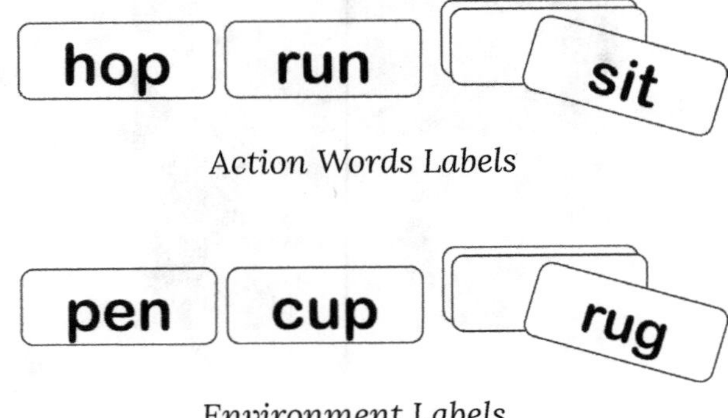

Action Words Labels

Environment Labels

Purpose: Decoding words without picture clues

Activity:

1. Take a card from the deck that is placed face down.
2. Decode the word and perform the action indicated by an Action Word Label or place the Environment Label on the object it describes.
3. Take another turn in order to model the game again.
4. Invite the student to take a turn and alternate turns as needed.

Notes:

- This is a great game for multiple students who take turns picking a card, decoding the word and performing the action or placing the label.
- The action labels can be used for a guessing game. A student reads a card and performs the action. The other students guess what word he has read.

3-Letter Word Lists

3-Letter Words	
cat	lip
bug	yes
top	fun
sit	jet
let	win
box	sun
hat	List 1

3-Letter Words	
cup	tip
red	dog
tan	egg
hop	bell
tell	get
hot	van
let	List 2

Purpose: Decoding practice without picture clues

Notes:

- Asking a student to practice a Word List card and then read it to you is a good assessment of the student's decoding skill.
- The student should be asked to return to these 3-letter word lists even when he has moved on to other, more advanced word clusters. Expect to see progress over time in the speed and accuracy with which the student decodes these words.
- With enough repetition and practice, you will see students begin to call out words automatically without "sounding out" each letter.
- Automatic word recognition will begin to happen naturally when students are given enough decoding practice.

4-Letter Word Activities

The following 4-letter word activities are to be displayed together in one area or on one shelf or tray. Images of these activities are on the self-checking practice sheets that students will use during independent practice sessions.

The teacher may include other 4-letter word activities she has found to be interesting and useful to her students.

Play blending and segmenting games with 4 phonemes to prepare the student for encoding and decoding activities with 4-letter short vowel words, which always have a blend at the beginning or at the end of the word (e.g. "**fl**ag," "**dr**ip," "fi**st**," "po**nd**"). For this reason, encoding and decoding 4-letter short vowel words requires more advanced phoneme segmentation and is harder than working with 3-letter short vowel words.

The child will already be very familiar with these 4-letter word activities because they are the same as the 3-letter activities. The games are not new but the challenge of working with 4 sounds and 4 letters is.

Introduce short vowel phrases once a student is successfully decoding 3 & 4-letter short vowel words.

4-Letter Word Pockets
Item #301

Prerequisite:

- The student can segment spoken words with 4 phonemes.
- The student has good recognition of the letters A to Z.

Purpose: Preparation for decoding 4-letter short vowel words

Activity:

1. Choose a word pocket. Remove the cards and place them neatly in a random order.
2. Identify the picture and segment the word into 4 phonemes.

   FLAG. */f/../l/../a/../g/.*
3. As you segment the word a second time, move the letter cards into the correct position left to right to build the word.
4. Move the letter cards back into a random order and ask the student to build *the same* word.

5. Invite the student to choose a word pocket and build a word.
6. Alternate turns as needed until he can work independently.

Notes:

- Encoding is the most powerful way to teach decoding.
- This "spelling" activity *is* reading instruction. It is reading instruction the student is giving himself, independent of the teacher.

4-Letter Word Puzzles
Item #341

Prerequisite:

- The student can segment spoken words with 4 phonemes.

- The student has good recognition of the letters A to Z.

Purpose:

- To match the sounds of a spoken word to printed letters
- Phoneme segmentation practice
- Direct preparation for decoding

Activity:

1. Take a card from the stack that is placed face-down.
2. Identify the picture and segment the word into 4 phonemes.

   NEST. */n/../e/../s/../t/.*

3. As you segment the word again, place transparent game pieces on the corresponding letters left to right.
4. Invite the student to take a turn and alternate turns as needed.

4-Letter Word Cards
Item #311

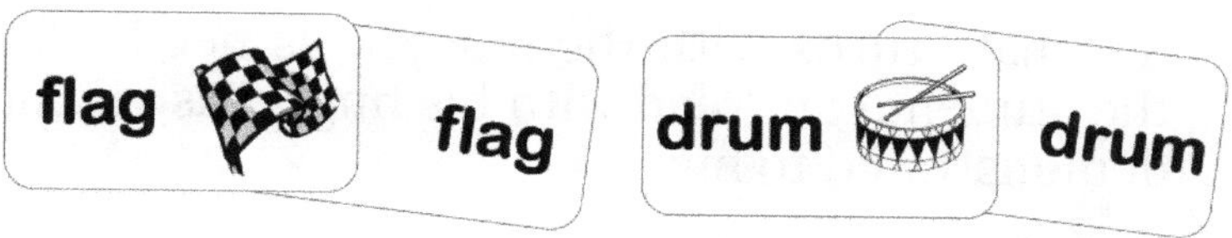

Prerequisites:

- The student can segment spoken words with 4 phonemes.

- The student has good recognition of the letters A to Z.

Purpose:

- To introduce decoding
- Phoneme segmentation practice
- Direct preparation for decoding

Activity #1:

1. Take a card from the stack that is placed face-down.
2. Identify the picture and segment the word into 4 phonemes.

   FLAG. */f/../l/../a/../g/.*

3. As you segment the word again, move your finger beneath the four letters from left to right. Then say the word as you touch the picture. You can say, "I *am reading with my finger*."
4. Invite the student to read the same card in the same manner.
5. Take another turn in order to model the process again.
6. Alternate turns with the student as needed until the student can "read with his finger" as you have demonstrated to him.

Notes:

1. The student is using phoneme segmentation to read the letters correctly.

2. This activity mimics what actual decoding looks like, sounds like, and feels like.

Activity #2:

1. The student holds the deck of cards near his chest so you can't see the pictures.
2. He "decodes" the word and you guess the hidden picture.

Challenge Activity:

1. Place the stack of word cards face down.
2. Decode the word on the top card then flip it over to see if you are right.
3. If you are right, the card is added to your personal stack. If you are incorrect, the card goes to the bottom of the stack.
4. Take another turn and then invite the student to take a turn.
5. Alternate turns as necessary until the student understands how to play the game.

Notes:

- Because the pictures are face down, the child is being asked to decode a word without any picture clue. He will get some right and he will get some wrong, but he has been well-prepared to tackle this decoding challenge. As he goes through this set multiple times, he gains greater accuracy and speed in reading letters and blending them quickly into the correct word.
- This is a perfect activity for a small group of students to play together.

4-Letter Pictures & Word Labels
Item #321

Prerequisites:

- The student can segment spoken words with 4 phonemes.
- The student has good recognition of the letters A to Z.

Purpose: Decoding practice

Activity:

1. Place the picture cards in a row left-to-right, giving the vocabulary of the pictures as you go.
2. Place the word labels in a column to the right of the picture cards.
3. Point to the first picture card, say the word and segment the sounds.

   NEST. */n/../e/../s/../t/.*

4. Search for the NEST label. Check that the letters on the label match the segmented sounds, then place the label beneath the picture.
5. Take another turn so the student clearly sees how you are playing the game—that you are starting with a picture card, then finding the letters that match the sounds of that word.

6. Invite the student to take a turn and alternate turns as needed.

Challenge Activity #1:

Ask the student to read the labels first and then place them beneath the correct picture.

Challenge Activity #2:

After the labels have been placed correctly, turn the picture cards face down and ask the student to read the labels without seeing the pictures. Turn over the picture cards to check your work as you go.

Note: This material should be divided into smaller sets of approximately 10 pictures and 10 labels. Otherwise there are too many individual pieces to keep the materials neatly organized on the workspace.

4-Letter Word Choice Game
Item #331

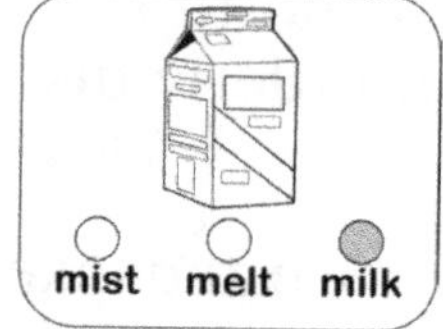

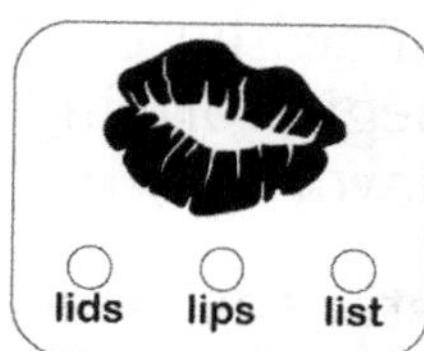

Prerequisites:

- The student can segment spoken words with 4 phonemes.
- The student has good recognition of the letters A to Z.

Purpose: Decoding practice

Activity:

1. Take a card from the stack that is placed face-down.
2. Identify the picture and segment the sounds.

   MILK. */m/../i/../l/../k/.*
3. Search for the word that says MILK, matching sounds to letters, starting with the word on the left, until you find the correct word.
4. Place the game piece in the circle above the answer.
5. Take another turn so the student clearly sees how you are playing the game—that you are starting with the picture, then finding the letters that match the sounds of that word.
6. Carefully slide the card to the top of the workspace to begin forming an orderly display of the completed work.
7. Invite the student to take a turn and take additional turns as needed.

4-Letter Action Words & Environment Labels

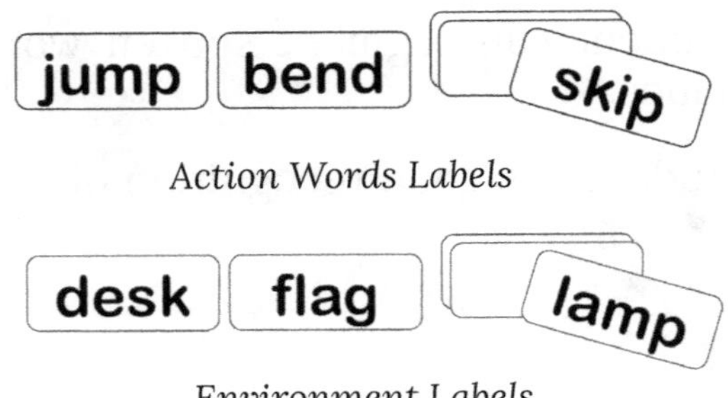

Action Words Labels

Environment Labels

Purpose: Decoding words without picture clues

Activity:

1. Take a card from the deck that is placed face down.
2. Decode the word and perform the action indicated by an Action Word Label or place the Environment Label on the object it describes.
3. Take another turn in order to model the game clearly.
4. Invite the student to take a turn and alternate turns as needed.

Notes:

- This is a great game for multiple students who take turns picking a card, decoding the word, and performing the action or placing the label.
- The action labels can be used for a guessing game. A student reads a card and performs the action. The other students guess what word he has read.

4-Letter Word Lists

4-Letter Words	
skip	crab
flag	swim
trap	frog
glad	plan
stop	trip
twin	flap
drum	List 1

4-Letter Words	
lamp	desk
mask	milk
tent	jump
list	lift
pond	hunt
gift	nest
fist	List 2

Purpose: Decoding practice without picture clues

Notes:

- Asking a student to practice a Word List card and then read it to you is a good assessment of the student's decoding skill.
- The student should be asked to return to these 4-letter word lists even when he has moved on to other, more advanced word clusters. Expect to see progress over time in the speed and accuracy with which the student decodes these words.
- With enough repetition and practice, you will see student begin to call out words automatically without "sounding out" each letter.
- Automatic word recognition will begin to happen naturally when students are given enough decoding practice.

5 & 6-Letter Word Activities

The following 5 & 6-letter word activities are to be displayed together in one area or on one shelf or tray. Images of these activities are on the self-checking practice sheets that students will use during independent practice sessions.

The teacher may include other 5 & 6-letter word activities she has found to be interesting and useful to her students.

The child will already be very familiar with these 5 & 6-letter word activities because they are the same ones as he has worked with previously. The games are not new, but the challenge of working with 5 or 6 sounds and letters is.

Work with phrases and sentences should continue parallel with these word activities.

5 & 6-Letter Word Pockets
Item #305

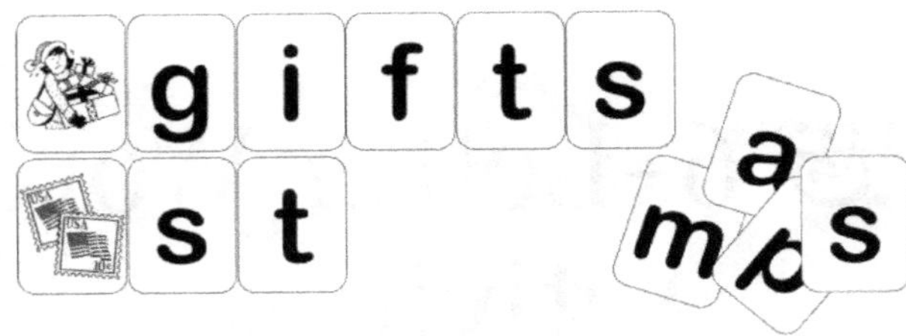

Prerequisite: The student has worked successfully with 4-letter word building and word reading activities.

Purpose: Preparation for decoding 5 & 6-letter short vowel words

Activity:

1. Choose a word pocket. Remove the cards and place them neatly in a random order.
2. Identify the picture and segment the word into its individual 5 or 6 phonemes.

   GIFTS. */g/../i/../f/../t/../s/.*
3. As you segment the word a second time, move the letter cards into the correct position left to right to build the word.
4. Move the letter cards back into a random order and ask the student to build *the same* word.
5. Invite the student to choose a word pocket and build a word.
6. Alternate turns as needed until he can work independently.

Notes:

- Segmenting a spoken word with 5 or 6 phonemes is quite difficult for a beginning reader. He may not necessarily segment each sound perfectly. But he has had many opportunities to build words and chances are very likely that he will form the word correctly, even if he doesn't discreetly segment each phoneme.
- Encoding is the most powerful way to teach decoding.
- This "spelling" activity *is* reading instruction. It is reading instruction the student is giving himself, independent of the teacher.

5 & 6-Letter Word Cards
Item #311

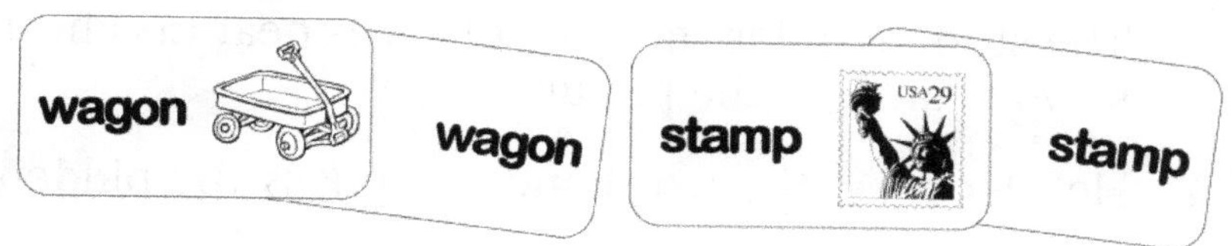

Prerequisite: The student has worked successfully with 4-letter word building and word reading activities.

Purpose: Decoding practice

Activity #1:

1. Take a card from the stack that is placed face-down.
2. Identify the picture and segment the word into its individual 5 or 6 phonemes.

   STAMP. */s/../t/../a/../m/../p/.*

3. As you segment the word again, move your finger beneath the three letters from left to right. Then say the word as you touch the picture. You can say, "*I am reading with my finger.*"

4. Invite the student to read the same card in the same manner.

5. Take another turn in order to model the process again.

6. Alternate turns with the student as needed until the student can "read with his finger" as you have demonstrated to him.

Note: The student is using phoneme segmentation to read the letters correctly.

Activity #2:

1. The student holds the deck of cards near his chest so you can't see the pictures.

2. He "decodes" the word and you guess the hidden picture.

Challenge Activity:

1. Place the stack of word cards face down.

2. Decode the word on the top card then flip it over to see if you are right.

3. If you are right, the card is added to your personal stack. If you are incorrect, the card goes to the bottom of the stack.

4. Take another turn and then invite the student to take a turn.

5. Alternate turns as necessary until the student understands how to play the game.

Notes:

- Because the pictures are face down, the child is being asked to decode a word without any picture clue. He will get some right and he will get some wrong, but he has been well-prepared to tackle this decoding challenge. As he goes through this set multiple times, he gains greater accuracy and speed in reading letters and blending them quickly into the correct word.
- This is a perfect activity for a small group of students to play together.

5 & 6-Letter Pictures & Word Labels
Item #322

Prerequisite: The student has worked successfully with 4-letter word building and word reading activities.

Purpose: Decoding practice

Activity:

1. Place the picture cards in a row left-to-right, giving the vocabulary of the pictures as you go.
2. Place the word labels in a column to the right of the picture cards.

3. Point to the first picture card, say the word and segment the sounds.

   STAMP. /s/../t/../a/../m/../p/.

4. Search for the STAMP label. Check that the letters on the label match the segmented sounds, then place the label beneath the picture.

5. Take another turn so the student clearly sees how you are playing the game—that you are starting with a picture card, then finding the letters that match the sounds of that word.

6. Invite the student to take a turn and alternate turns as needed.

Challenge Activity #1: Ask the student to read the labels first and then place them beneath the correct picture.

Challenge Activity #2: After the labels have been placed correctly, turn the picture cards face down and ask the student to read the labels without seeing the pictures. Turn over the picture cards to check your work as you go.

Note: This material should be divided into smaller sets of approximately 10 pictures and 10 labels. Otherwise there are too many individual pieces to keep the materials neatly organized on the workspace.

5 & 6-Letter Word Choice Game
Item #335

Prerequisite: The student has worked successfully with 4-letter word building and word reading activities.

Purpose: Decoding practice

Activity:

1. Take a card from the stack that is placed face-down.
2. Identify the picture and segment the sounds.

   PLANT. */p/../l/../a/../n/../t/.*
3. Search for the word that says PLANT, matching sounds to letters, starting with the word on the left, until you find the correct word.
4. Place the game piece in the circle above the answer.
5. Take another turn so the student clearly sees how you are playing the game—that you are starting with the picture, then finding the letters that match the sounds of that word.
6. Carefully slide the card to the top of the work-space to begin forming an orderly display of the completed work.
7. Invite the student to take a turn and take additional turns as needed.

5 & 6-Letter Word Lists

5 & 6-Letter Words	
stamp	lemon
swift	wagon
clamp	plums
twigs	twins
trunk	swing
robin	plant
hat	List 1

5 & 6-Letter Words	
seven	picnic
camel	insect
splat	plugs
helmet	juggle
skunk	rocket
clips	gifts
tunnel	List 2

Purpose: Decoding practice without picture clues

Notes:

- Asking a student to practice a Word List and then read it to you is a good assessment of the student's decoding skill.
- The student should be asked to return to these 5 & 6-letter word lists even when he has moved on to other, more advanced word clusters. Expect to see progress over time in the speed and accuracy with which the student decodes these words.
- With enough repetition and practice, you will see students begin to call out words automatically without "sounding out" each letter.
- Automatic word recognition will begin to happen naturally when students are given enough decoding practice.

Short Vowel Phrases & Sentences

Work with short vowel phrases should begin once a student is successfully decoding 3 & 4-letter short vowel words.

Students will need to learn a set of high frequency words in order to read phrases and sentences.

High Frequency (Dolch) Words Set 1

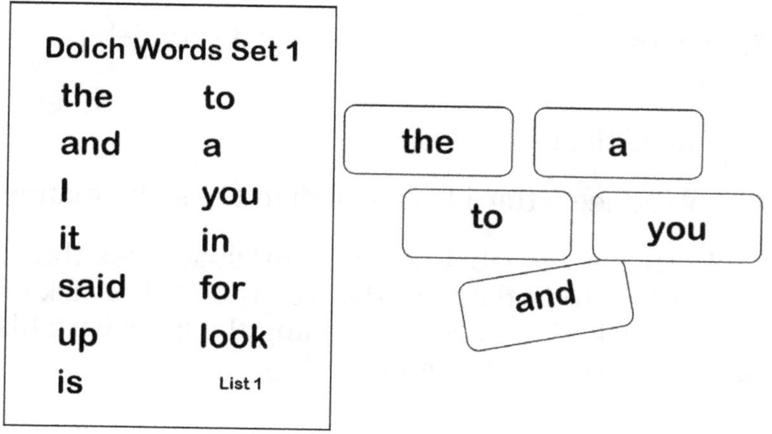

Activity:

1. Place a Dolch word label on the workspace in front of the student.
2. Say the word and then decode the word sound-by-sound as you move your fingers below each letter or letter team (phonogram).

   YOU. */y/../oo/* YOU.

3. Ask the student to "read" the word in the same manner.

   Read the word YOU.

4. Place a second Dolch word label on the work-space. Say the word and then decode the word sound-by-sound, using your finger in the same manner as before.

   TO. */t/../oo/* TO.

5. Ask the student to read the word sound-by-sound.

   Read the word TO.

6. Introduce a third Dolch label in the same manner.
7. With 3 Dolch labels on the workspace, ask the student to find one of the words and then ask him to check his answer by reading the label with his finger sound-by-sound.

   Find the word TO.
   Good. Now read the word TO.

8. Mix up the word labels and ask the student to find another word.

Show me the word AND.
Good. Now read the word AND.

9. After working with the three labels in this manner, ask the student to read a word he knows.
10. Ask him to "check his answer" by sounding out the word. This will reinforce the spelling pattern of the word, which will likely contain a letter combination he has not yet encountered, like "ou."
11. Continue to introduce additional Dolch words as a regular part of your reading instruction and play simple games to increase familiarity with these high frequency words.
12. Use the Dolch Word List Cards for practice and for evaluation of the student's progress.

Notes:

- Many of the Dolch words have letter combinations (phonograms) and spelling patterns the student has not yet learned. But a word label you have asked him to "decode" is a word you have already identified *for* him. Thus, when he decodes, he is actually segmenting the spoken word and then mapping those sounds onto the letters of the printed word. In other words, the student already knows what word he is being asked to decode. Because he is moving from the *known* to the *unknown*, this is more of a *matching* activity than a decoding activity.
- This approach is a much more productive way of introducing and teaching these high frequency words than using a flash card method. This approach reinforces the student's phoneme

segmentation and letter recognition while introducing him to new spelling patterns.

- Teaching Dolch high frequency words now becomes a regular part of weekly reading instruction.

Short Vowel Phrases: Pictures & Labels
Item #400

Activity:

1. Place the picture cards in a row left-to-right at the top of the workspace as you say the words printed on the labels the student will be reading.

    a lot of gifts
    sad men
    a fat pig
    etc.

2. Choose a label, read it and place it beneath the correct picture.

3. Take several turns in order to model the reading of connected text.

4. Invite the student to take a turn then alternate turns as necessary until the student can be independent with this activity.

Challenge Activity #1: Ask the student to read the labels first and then place them beneath the correct picture.

Challenge Activity #2: After the labels have been placed correctly, turn the picture cards face down and have the student read the labels without seeing the pictures. Turn over the picture cards to check your work as you go.

Notes:

- When the student reads a phrase label, you can expect to hear a combination of the decoding letter-by-letter of some words, and the automatic recognition of others.
- This material should be divided into smaller sets of approximately 10 picture cards and 10 labels. Otherwise there are too many individual pieces to keep them neatly organized on the workspace.

Short Vowel Phrases: Practice Lists

Short Vowel Phrases

a hot sun
a fast dog
cups of milk
the red bus
six kids
a fat cat

List 1

Short Vowel Phrases

ten fat cats
a lot of fun
a lost dog
the red bus
spin the top
the last bun

List 2

Purpose: Decoding practice without picture clues

Notes:

- Asking a student to practice a list of Short Vowel Phrases and then read it to you is a good assessment of the student's ability to begin reading connected text.

- The student should be asked to return to these phrase cards even when he has moved on to other, more advanced activities. Expect to see progress over time in the speed and accuracy with which the student decodes these phrases.
- Students will continue to advance in their ability to call out words automatically without decoding each letter.

Short Vowel Sentences: Pictures & Sentence Labels Item #410

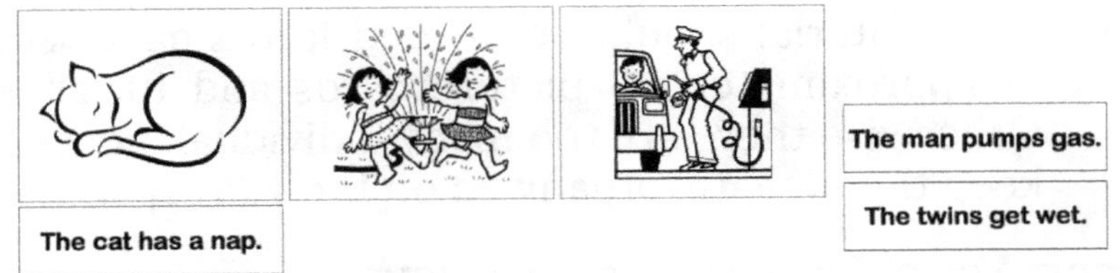

Activity:

1. Place the picture cards in a row left-to-right at the top of the workspace as you say the words printed on the labels the student will be reading.

   The cat has a nap.
   The twins get wet.
   The man pumps gas.
   etc.

2. Choose a sentence label, read it and place it beneath the correct picture.
3. Take several turns in order to model the reading of connected text.
4. Invite the student to take a turn, then alternate turns as necessary until the student can work independently.

Note: This material should be divided into smaller sets of approximately 10 picture cards and 10 labels.

Otherwise there are too many individual pieces to keep them neatly organized on the workspace.

Short Vowel Sentences: Yes. No. Maybe So. Item #411

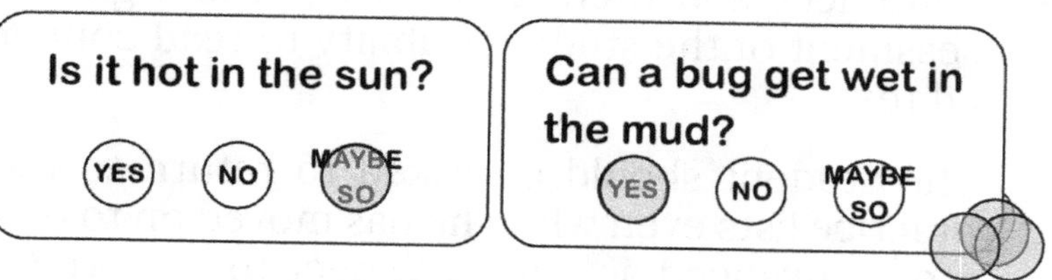

Purpose: Independent sentence reading practice without picture clues

Activity:

1. Student #1 chooses a Yes. No. Maybe So. card and reads it to another student.
2. Student #2 answers "Yes" or "No" or "Maybe so" and gives his reasoning.

Note: Each student is bound to have differing answers and unique reasoning. Fun discussion, hilarious dialogue and earnest disagreements ensue, leading to much repetition.

Short Vowel Sentences: Practice Lists

Short Vowel Sentences

Can I have a dog?
I like to sip milk.
She will help us.
My hat is black.
It is a big box.
The flag is up.

List 1

Short Vowel Sentences

The cat is on the bed.
I will pet the soft cat.
Dad fed the six pigs.
Tim runs fast to the bus.
The dog is on the rug.
A fox sat next to a tent.

List 2

Purpose: Decoding practice without picture clues

Notes:

- Asking a student to practice a list of Short Vowel Sentences and then read it to you is a good assessment of the student's ability to read connected text.
- The student should be asked to return to these practice lists even when he has moved on to other, more advanced activities. Expect to see progress over time in the speed and accuracy with which the student decodes these sentences.
- Students will continue to advance in their ability to call out words automatically without decoding each letter.

High Frequency (Dolch) Words Set 2

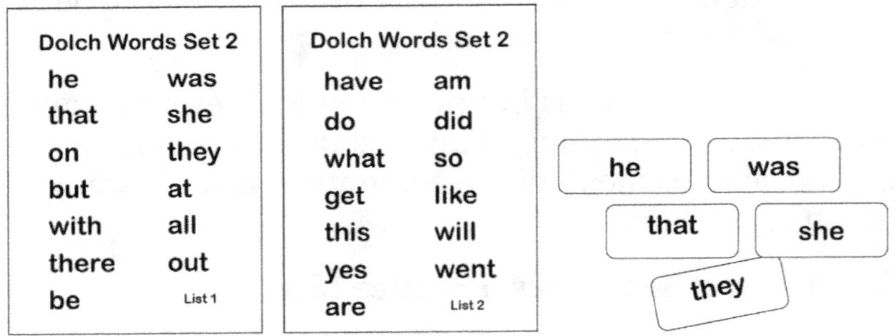

Activity:

1. Place a Dolch word label on the workspace in front of the student.
2. Say the word and then decode the word sound-by-sound as you move your fingers below each letter or letter team.

   HE. */h/../ē/*. HE.

3. Ask the student to "read" the word in the same manner.

   Read the word HE.

4. Place a second Dolch word label on the workspace. Say the word and then decode the word sound-by-sound, using your finger in the same manner as before.

   THAT. */th/../a/../t/.* THAT.

5. Ask the student to read the word sound-by-sound. Read the word THAT.

6. Introduce a third Dolch label in the same manner.

7. With 3 Dolch labels on the workspace, ask the student to find one of the words and then ask him to check his answer by reading the label with his finger sound-by-sound.

   Find the word HE.
   Good.
   Now read the word HE.

8. Mix up the word labels and ask the student to find another word.

   Show me the word THAT.
   Good. Now read the word THAT.

9. After working with the three labels in this manner, ask the student to read a word he knows.

10. Ask him to "check his answer" by sounding out the word. This reinforces the spelling pattern of the word, which will likely contain a letter combination he has not yet encountered, like "ou."

11. Continue to introduce additional Dolch words as a regular part of your reading instruction and play

simple games to increase familiarity with these high frequency words.

12. Use the Dolch Word List Cards for practice and for evaluation of the student's progress.

Notes:

- Many of the Dolch words have letter combinations (phonograms) and spelling patterns the student has not yet learned. But a word label you have asked him to "decode" is a word you have already identified for him. Thus, when he decodes, he is actually segmenting the spoken word and then mapping those sounds onto the letters of the printed word. In other words, the student already knows what word he is being asked to decode. Because he is moving from the *known* to the *unknown*, this is more of a *matching* activity than a decoding activity.

- This approach is a much more productive way of introducing and teaching these high frequency words than using a flash card method. This approach reinforces the student's phoneme segmentation and letter recognition while introducing him to new spelling patterns.

- Teaching Dolch high frequency words continues to be a regular part of weekly reading instruction.

Dolch Sentences: Yes. No. Maybe So.
Item #412

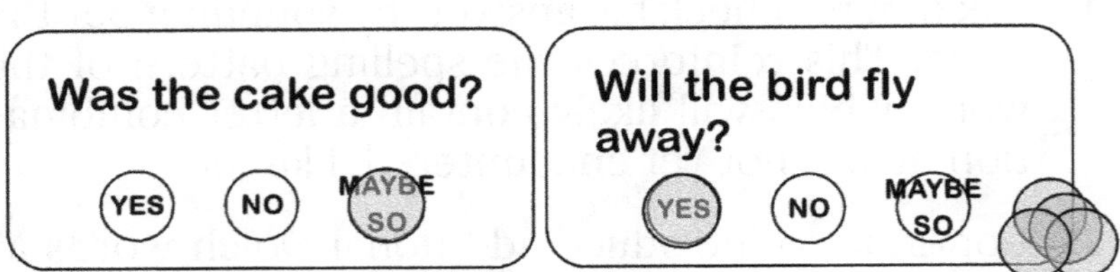

Purpose: Independent sentence reading practice without picture clues

Activity:

1. Student #1 chooses a Yes. No. Maybe So. card and reads it to another student.
2. Student #2 answers "Yes" or "No" or "Maybe so" and gives his reasoning.

Notes:

- These short sentences contain both highly decodable short vowel words and high frequency (Dolch) words, which pose a more difficult challenge.
- Each student is bound to have differing answers and unique reasoning. Fun discussion, hilarious dialogue and earnest disagreements ensue, leading to much repetition.

Dolch Sentences: Practice Lists

Dolch Sentences

I can ride a fast horse.

She will read a good book.

He has all the candy.

The bird is in the tree.

I fell down the big hill.

The girls game home.

List 1

Dolch Sentences

What is in the cake?

They want a new cat.

The dog ran away.

Mom went away with

Look at my pretty dress.

He went to school today.

List 2

Purpose: Decoding more difficult sentences without picture clues

Notes:

- Asking a student to practice a list of sentences and then read it to you is a good assessment of the student's ability to read connected text that includes both short vowel decodable words and high frequency (Dolch) words.
- The student should be asked to return to these phrase cards even when he has moved on to other, more advanced activities. Expect to see progress over time in the speed and accuracy with which the student decodes these sentences.
- Students will continue to advance in their ability to call out words automatically without decoding each letter.

Decodable Readers

Decodable books contain words with letter combinations and spelling patterns that a student has learned. A small number of high-frequency words are also used. As a student learns new elements of the alphabetic code, the vocabulary used in the decodable books expands to include new spelling patterns and phonograms.

It is important that the decodable text matches the sequence of instruction in letter-sounds and spelling patterns that are taught throughout an early reading program, especially for struggling readers.

Using decodable text in the earlier stages of reading instruction ensures that a student has the knowledge and skills to read stories without guessing. They are especially important for the struggling reader who is often asked to read books that are beyond his abilities, which reinforces a sense of failure he experiences on a daily basis.

Reading decodable text helps students build fluency and gain confidence as they become proficient with decoding.

Decodable books are needed until the student is able to decode unfamiliar words easily and can tackle more authentic, age-appropriate text found in leveled readers.

Example of Decodable Reader Sets

Primary Phonics Readers Set 1

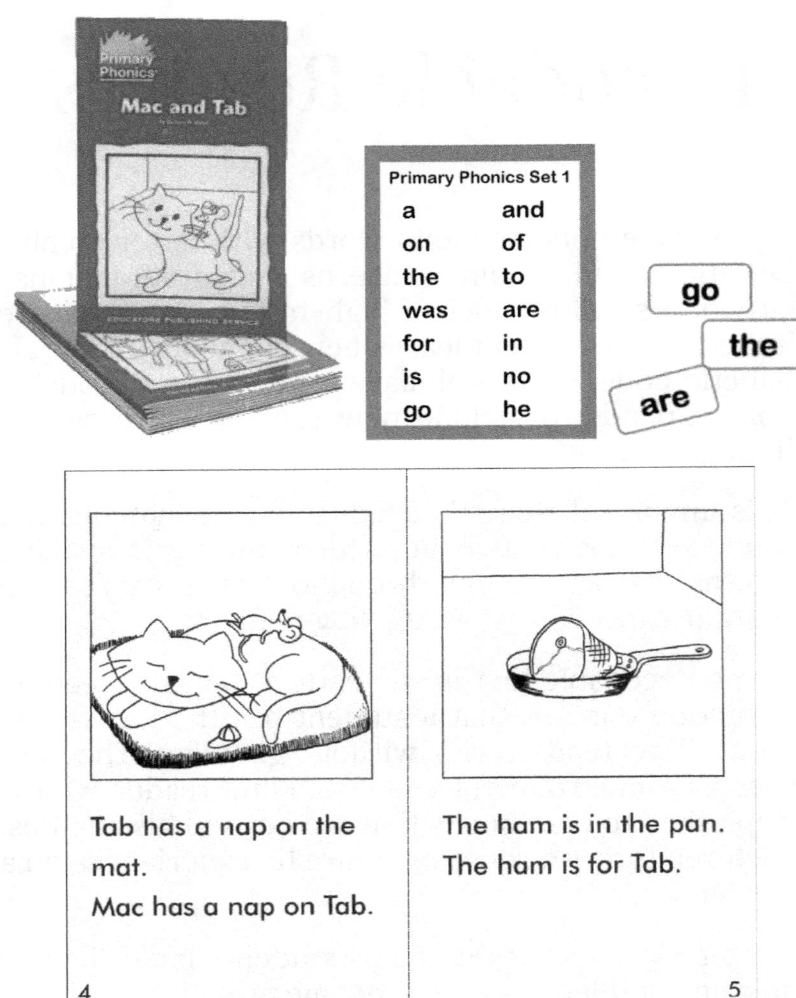

Primary Phonics Readers Set 2

Primary Phonics Readers Set 3

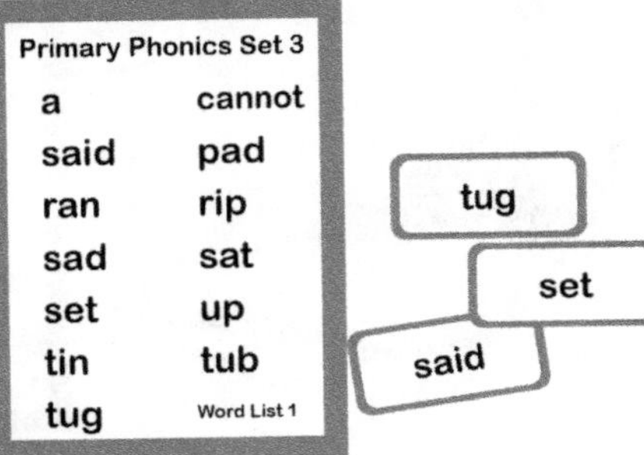
Primary Phonics Set 3

a	cannot
said	pad
ran	rip
sad	sat
set	up
tin	tub
tug	Word List 1

New Spelling Patterns and Phonograms

The encoding and decoding activities below will be very familiar to the student and are designed to introduce new spelling patterns and phonograms.

The student will apply excellent phoneme segmentation skills, strong alphabet knowledge and confident decoding ability to figure out words with unfamiliar letter combinations and spelling patterns.

The teacher guides the student to start with the *picture* with each activity. Segmenting the sounds of the picture prompts the child to find the letter or letters that match those sounds to the correct word.

In this way, the student will begin to teach himself *how* to figure out unfamiliar words.

Silent E Words

Silent E Word Pockets
Item #302

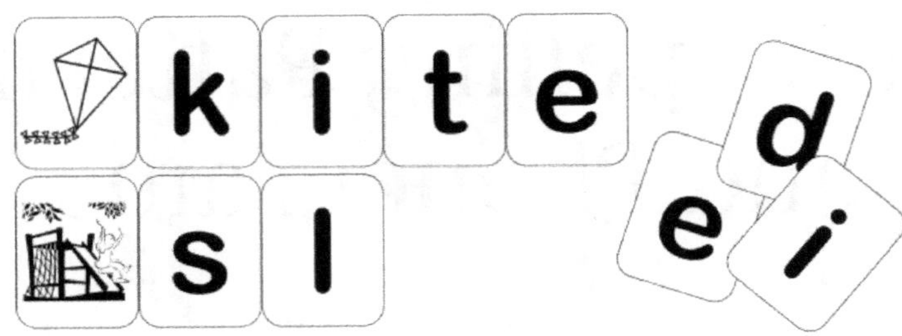

Purpose: Preparation for decoding words that have a silent E that makes the vowel "say its name"

Activity:

1. Choose a word pocket. Remove the cards and place them neatly in a random order.
2. Identify the picture and segment the word into 4 phonemes.

   SLIDE. */s/../l/../ī/../d/.*

3. As you segment the word a second time, move the letter cards into the correct position left to right to build the word.
4. There are 5 letter cards but only 4 phonemes, but the Silent E card will need to be in its place in order for the word to spell SLIDE.

   This says SLID*, but when I move the* E *to the end, it will say* SLIDE.
   This is a Silent E. *It doesn't say anything, but it makes the letter "i" say its name.*

5. Move the letter cards back into a random order and ask the student to build the same word.

6. Invite the student to choose a word pocket and build a word.

7. Alternate turns as needed until he can work independently.

Notes:

- Encoding is the most powerful way to teach decoding.

- This "spelling" activity ***is*** reading instruction—reading instruction the student is giving himself, independent of the teacher.

Silent E Word Cards
Item #312

Purpose:

- Phoneme segmentation practice
- Practice decoding Silent E words

Activity #1:

1. Take a card from the stack that is placed face-down.
2. Identify the picture and segment the word into 3 or 4 phonemes.

   SKATE. /s/../k/../ā/../t/.

3. As you segment the word again, move your finger beneath the letters from left to right. You will *not* put your finger beneath the letter E, because it is silent.
4. Say the word as you touch the picture. *I am reading with my finger.*
5. Invite the student to read the same card in the same manner.
6. Take another turn in order to model the process again.
7. Alternate turns with the student as needed until the student can "read with his finger" as you have demonstrated to him.

Notes:

- The student is using phoneme segmentation to read the letters correctly.
- This activity mimics what actual decoding looks like, sounds like and feels like.

Activity #2:

1. The student holds the deck of cards near his chest so you can't see the pictures.
2. He "decodes" the word and you guess the hidden picture.

Challenge Activity:

1. Place the stack of word cards face down.
2. Decode the word on the top card then flip it over to see if you are right.
3. If you are right, the card is added to your personal stack. If you are incorrect, the card goes to the bottom of the stack.
4. Take another turn and then invite the student to take a turn.
5. Alternate turns as necessary until the student understands how to play the game.

Notes:

- Because the pictures are face down, the child is being asked to decode a word without any picture clues. He will get some right and he will get some wrong, but he has been well-prepared to tackle this decoding challenge. And as he goes through this set multiple times, he gains greater accuracy and speed in reading letters and blending them quickly into the correct word.
- This is a perfect activity for a small group of students to play together.

Silent E Pictures & Word Labels
Item #323

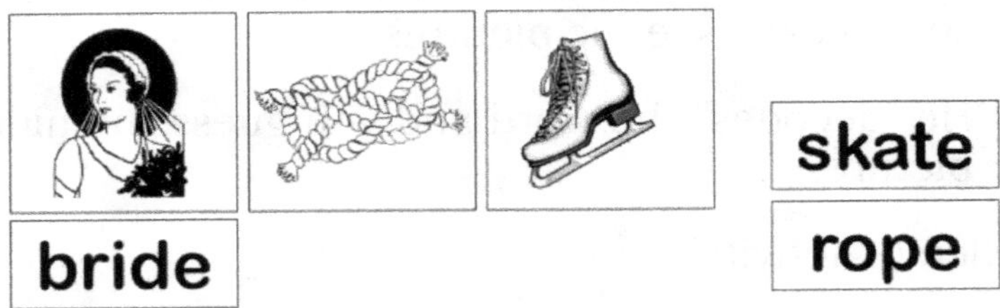

Activity:

1. Place the picture cards in a row left-to-right, giving the vocabulary of the pictures as you go.
2. Place the word labels in a column to the right of the picture cards.
3. Point to the first picture card, say the word and segment the sounds.

   BRIDE. */b/../r/../ī/../d/.*

4. Search for the BRIDE label. Check that the letters on the label match the segmented sounds, then place the label beneath the picture.
5. Take another turn so the student clearly sees how you are playing the game—that you are starting with a picture card, then finding the letters that match the sounds of that word.
6. Invite the student to take a turn and alternate turns as needed.

Challenge Activity #1: Ask the student to read the labels first and then place them beneath the correct picture.

Challenge Activity #2: After the labels have been placed correctly, turn the picture cards face down and ask the student to read the labels without seeing the pictures. Turn over the picture cards to check your work as you go.

Note: This material should be divided into smaller sets of approximately 10 pictures and 10 labels. Otherwise there are too many individual pieces to keep the materials neatly organized on the workspace.

Silent E Word Choice
Item #336

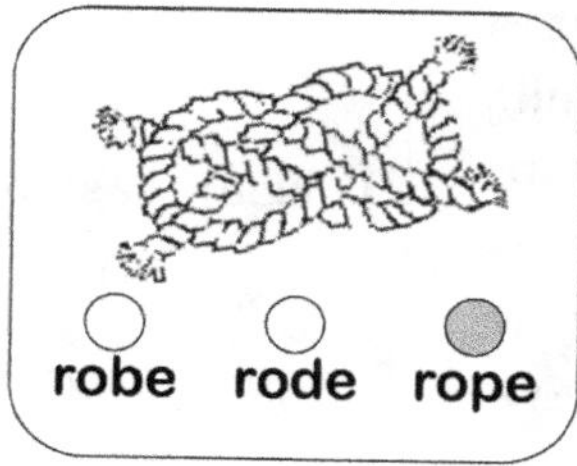

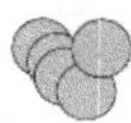

Activity:

1. Take a card from the stack that is placed face-down.
2. Identify the picture and segment the sounds.

   ROPE. */r/../ō/../p/.*

3. Search for the word that says ROPE, matching sounds to letters, starting with the word on the left, until you find the correct word.
4. Place the game piece in the circle above the answer.
5. Take another turn so the student clearly sees how you are playing the game—that you are starting with the picture, then finding the letters that match the sounds of that word.

6. Carefully slide the card to the top of the workspace to begin forming an orderly display of the completed work.

7. Invite the student to take a turn and take additional turns as needed.

Silent E Word Lists

Purpose: Practice decoding Silent E words without picture clues

Notes:

- Asking a student to practice a Silent E word list card and then read it to you is a good assessment of the student's decoding skill.

- The student should be asked to return to these Silent E word lists even when he has moved on to other, more advanced word clusters. Expect to see progress over time in the speed and accuracy with which the student decodes these words.

- With enough repetition and practice, you will see students begin to call out words automatically without "sounding out" each letter.

- Automatic word recognition will begin to happen naturally when students are given enough decoding practice.

Phonograms

Up to this point the student has learned single letters that represent a single sound. Now we will present activities that teach letter combinations—or phonograms—that also represent one sound.

For example:

"OA" is a phonogram that says /ō/ as in GOAT.

"SH" is a phonogram that says /sh/ as in SHIP.

The great majority of multi-letter phonograms are very regular in the sounds they represent. A study of 17,000 words showed that most words follow the regular phonogram sounds. Only 3% of the words are completely irregular, like "said".

Remember that these activities do not ask the child to read letters—especially unfamiliar multi-letter phonograms—but only to recognize or choose them when prompted by a sound.

Phonogram Word Pockets
Item #303

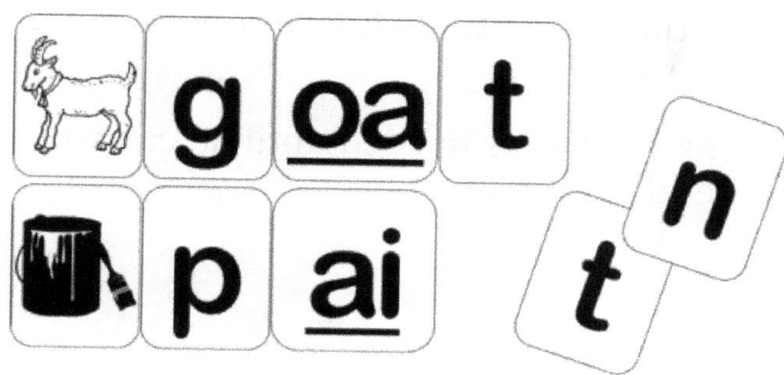

Purpose: Preparation for decoding words that have a 2-letter spelling pattern that represents one sound.

Activity:

1. Choose a word pocket. Remove the cards and place them neatly in a random order.
2. Identify the picture and segment the word into 3 or 4 phonemes.

   PAINT. */p/../ā/../n/../t/.*

3. As you segment the word a second time, move the letter cards into the correct position left to right to build the word.
4. Move the letter cards back into a random order and ask the student to build the same word.
5. Invite the student to choose a word pocket and build a word.
6. Alternate turns as needed until he can work independently.

Notes:

- Encoding is the most powerful way to teach decoding.
- This "spelling" activity ***is*** reading instruction—reading instruction the student is giving himself, independent of the teacher.

Phonogram Word Cards
Item #313

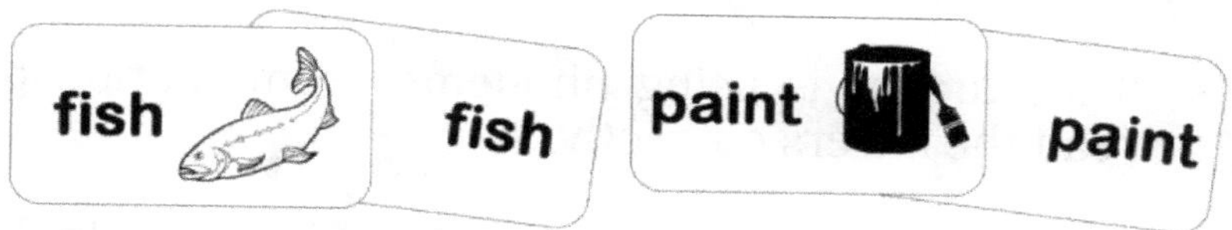

Purpose: Preparation for decoding words with 2-letter phonograms

Activity #1:

1. Take a card from the stack that is placed face-down.

2. Identify the picture and segment the word into individual phonemes.

   FISH. */f/../i/../sh/.*

3. As you segment the word again, move your finger beneath the letters from left to right. You will put your finger beneath and in the middle of a 2-letter phonogram that makes one sound.

4. Say the word as you touch the picture.

   I am reading with my finger.

5. Invite the student to read the same card in the same manner.

6. Take another turn in order to model the process again.

7. Alternate turns with the student as needed until the student can "read with his finger" as you have demonstrated to him.

Notes:

- The student is using phoneme segmentation to read the letters correctly.

- This activity mimics what actual decoding looks like, sounds like and feels like.

Activity #2:

1. The student holds the deck of cards near his chest so you can't see the pictures.

2. He "decodes" the word and you guess the hidden picture.

Challenge Activity:

1. Place the stack of word cards face down.

2. Decode the word on the top card then flip it over to see if you are right.

3. If you are right, the card is added to your personal stack. If you are incorrect, the card goes to the bottom of the stack.

4. Take another turn and then invite the student to take a turn.

5. Alternate turns as necessary until the student understands how to play the game.

Notes:

- Because the pictures are face down, the child is being asked to decode a word without any picture clues. He will get some right and he will get some wrong, but he has been well-prepared to tackle this decoding challenge. And as he goes through this set multiple times, he gains greater accuracy and speed in reading letters and blending them quickly into the correct word.

- This is a perfect activity for a small group of students to play together.

Phonogram Pictures & Word Labels
Item #324

Activity:

1. Place the picture cards in a row left-to-right, giving the vocabulary of the pictures as you go.

2. Place the word labels in a column to the right of the picture cards.

3. Point to the first picture card, say the word and segment the sounds.

   BIRD. */b/../ir/../d/.*

4. Search for the BIRD label. Check that the letters on the label match the segmented sounds, then place the label beneath the picture.

5. Take another turn so the student clearly sees how you are playing the game—that you are starting with a picture card, then finding the letters that match the sounds of that word.

6. Invite the student to take a turn and alternate turns as needed.

Challenge Activity #1: Ask the student to read the labels first and then place them beneath the correct picture.

Challenge Activity #2: After the labels have been placed correctly, turn the picture cards face down and ask the student to read the labels without seeing the pictures. Turn over the picture cards to check your work as you go.

Note: This material should be divided into smaller sets of approximately 10 pictures and 10 labels. Otherwise there are too many individual pieces to keep the materials neatly organized on the workspace.

Phonogram Word Choice
Item #337

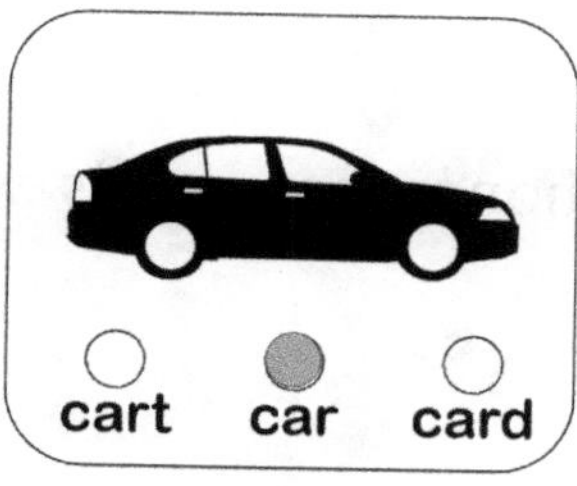

Activity:

1. Take a card from the stack that is placed face-down.
2. Identify the picture and segment the sounds.

   CLOWN. */c/../l/../ow/../n/.*
3. Search for the word that says CLOWN, matching sounds to letters, starting with the word on the left, until you find the correct word.
4. Place the game piece in the circle above the answer.
5. Carefully slide the card to the top of the work-space to begin forming an orderly display of the completed work.
6. Take another turn so the student clearly sees how you are playing the game—that you are starting with the picture, then finding the letters that match the sounds of that word.
7. Carefully slide the card to the top of the work-space to begin forming an orderly display of the completed work.

8. Invite the student to take a turn and take additional turns as needed.

Phonogram Word Lists

Purpose: Practice decoding phonogram words without picture clues

Notes:

- Asking a student to practice a phonogram word list card and then read it to you is a good assessment of the student's decoding skill.
- The student should be asked to return to these phonogram word lists even when he has moved on to other, more advanced word clusters. Expect to see progress over time in the speed and accuracy with which the student decodes these words.
- With enough repetition and practice, you will see students begin to call out words automatically without "sounding out" each letter.
- Automatic word recognition will begin to happen naturally when students are given enough decoding practice.

ch	
chin	chip
punch	chop
chat	such
chick	ranch
chill	chum
punch	chant
rich	lunch

ee	
bee	sleep
weep	freeze
peel	jeep
sweet	tree
heel	seed
meet	street
breeze	green

Notes:

- The key picture at the top of each Phonogram Word List Card introduces the student to the new spelling pattern.
- For example, the picture of CHAIR tells him the new phonogram makes the sound /ch/.
- He can figure out the sound of the phonogram EE by the picture of the BEE.

Phonogram Words	
seal	tree
soap	deer
corn	jeep
goat	leaf
fork	shell
horn	sail
nail	List 1

Phonogram Words	
cow	crow
sleep	bird
nurse	ship
owl	house
mouse	fish
train	clown
snail	List 2

Notes:

- Each word on the lists above contains only one irregular spelling pattern. Plus the student has encountered these words from previous phonogram work. Thus, decoding these words without picture clues will not be difficult for the student.
- The vocabulary of the words on the list are familiar to a young child and the reading skills he has developed thus far will serve him well and help him figure out most, if not all, of the words. Asking a student to practice a phonogram word list card and then read it to you is a good assessment of the student's decoding skill.

Classified Vocabulary

The following are examples of the kind of reading material you can introduce to students who are very good at decoding and gaining mastery in figuring out new words.

It is best to begin with vocabulary that is already familiar to the student. If he recognizes a picture of a wolf, then he can search for the word label that says WOLF. By segmenting the word WOLF, he can check those sounds against the letters in the printed word. That doesn't mean he can read the word WOLF tomorrow, but he will have the experience of encountering a new (and unusual) spelling pattern and seeing how it maps to sounds in a word he knows.

Through these classified vocabulary activities, the student will gain great strength in the core reading skills that he will then apply to unfamiliar words he will encounter every day.

He may or may not have previously learned the phonogram EE, as in SHEEP, but his subconscious mind will start to put together information he is gleaning from unfamiliar words he is successfully matching to familiar pictures.

Teachers should introduce the vocabulary of pictures that may be unfamiliar to students and teach students how to politely ask the names of unfamiliar pictures in any of the classified vocabulary sets.

This is advanced word reading that the student can begin while he is working with decodable readers and leveled readers.

Classified Vocabulary: Animals of North America

Classified Vocabulary: Farm Animals

Classified Vocabulary: Kinds of Transportation

Leveled Readers

A leveled book collection is a set of books organized in levels of difficulty from easy books for an emergent reader to longer, more complex books that advanced readers will select. There can be as many as ten levels for grades K–1 and three or four levels for each later grade.

Leveled readers typically have simple plots and some repetition. Beginning books use high-frequency words as well as short vowel easy-to-decode words. They also provide pictures to support the reader in gaining meaning and identifying words. Beginning leveled readers start with simple sentences and may only have three or four sentences per page. Topics and themes will be familiar to the young student.

Leveled readers are the student's entry into authentic reading, i.e. text that is not solely based on short vowel decodable words.

Leveled readers are the student's entry into authentic reading, i.e. text that is not solely based on short vowel decodable words.

Having increasing levels of difficulty provides a way to evaluate children's progress over time.

A book collection is established that does not need to be replaced but is revised and expanded over time.

Leveled reader sets must be a part of the instructional environment.

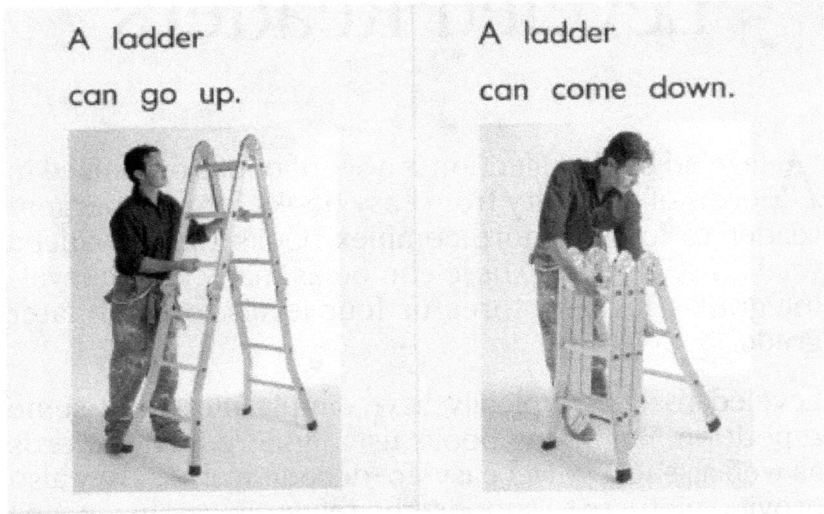

Example of a Beginning Leveled Reader

Appendix A

Program Overview

The activities in this program give beginning and struggling readers a concrete understanding of the alphabetic principle, strong letter knowledge, confident decoding, and fluency with connected text in sentences and books. Most importantly this method teaches children how to teach themselves to read.

1. Teach beginning sound isolation through activities that model the isolation of the beginning sounds of spoken words. Example: /b/..BALL; /sh/..SHIP.
2. Provide activities for independent beginning sound isolation practice.
3. Teach phoneme blending and segmentation through activities that model the breaking apart of spoken words into individual phonemes.
4. Introduce the alphabetic principle by showing the child how to identify the sound of a letter that is next to a picture. Example: BEAR begins with the sound /b/. The child isolates the beginning sound of BEAR to identify the sound of the letter “b”.
5. Provide a sequence of self-directed activities for learning the alphabet, organized by letter clusters.

6. Introduce decoding and provide a sequence of self-directed activities—organized by difficulty—that provide repetition and practice necessary for decoding mastery. Word activity clusters move from easy (3-letter) to harder (4-letter) to still harder (5 & 6-letter) short vowel words. Additional word clusters will teach new spelling patterns.

7. Teach a beginning set of high frequency (Dolch) words and introduce materials for decoding connected text in short vowel phrases and sentences.

8. Provide sets of decodable readers.

9. Provide materials and reading activities that guide students to apply alphabet knowledge and decoding skills to new spelling patterns and multi-letter phonograms. Examples: AI as in TRAIN; OA as in BOAT; Silent E as in KITE, etc.)

10. Provide advanced word reading activities with classified vocabulary materials.

11. Introduce leveled readers and continue to teach Dolch high frequency words.

Appendix B

Principles of Teaching Children How to Teach Themselves to Read

- Children in large part teach themselves to read from the instruction and activities we provide them. They learn how to figure out things on their own, like unfamiliar phonograms and new spelling patterns.
- The application of the alphabetic principle to identify letters and words is the basis of all the activities in this method and it is how the child will teach himself to read.
- Effective early reading instruction is based on activities that guide the student from *speech* to *print*, from *sound* to *symbol* and which move from the *concrete* to the *abstract*.
- Teach the alphabetic principle before you teach the alphabet.
- The foundation of alphabet mastery is beginning sound isolation.
- Letter knowledge is best learned by the child through his application of the alphabetic principle using self-guided materials to match beginning sounds to printed letters.

- The foundation of reading and spelling words is phoneme segmentation, the most important beginning reading skill. Struggling readers often lack this ability to separate spoken words into individual sounds.

- Decoding skills are best learned by the child through his application of the alphabetic principle using self-guided materials to match sounds of spoken words to letters in printed words.

- The organization of materials in the environment is crucial in implementing effective early reading instruction. The various games and activities for each skill level are grouped together in an attractive manner and made easily accessible to students. This helps to structure the learning environment so that students understand which games they may freely choose to work with.

- Freedom to choose is key to gradually shifting responsibility for learning to the student.

- Freedom to choose individualizes the learning experience for the student according to his strengths and interests.

- Teaching is not testing. Don't ask a student a question unless you are sure he knows the answer. If the child gives a wrong answer, that means you've asked the wrong question. If you give him a choice of answers, he will usually choose the right one.

- Repetition is the teacher's best teaching tool and the quickest, most direct way for a student to master skills and information. Repetition is the healing balm of education.

- Emphasis must shift from a traditional model of memorization through drill, to a deeper, more permanent learning through self-guided hands-on activities.
- Do not do for the child what he can do for himself.

Early Reading Mastery Classroom in Midrand South Africa.

Appendix C

Student Self-Checking Practice Sheets

The use of self-checking practice sheets is an important element of the self-guided learning process and helps students share in the responsibility of learning. Each sheet is a different activity cluster with pictures of the various games a student can choose to work with. Next to each game image are little boxes to be checked when he has practiced that activity. A child may not necessarily need to check each box before moving on in the sequence.

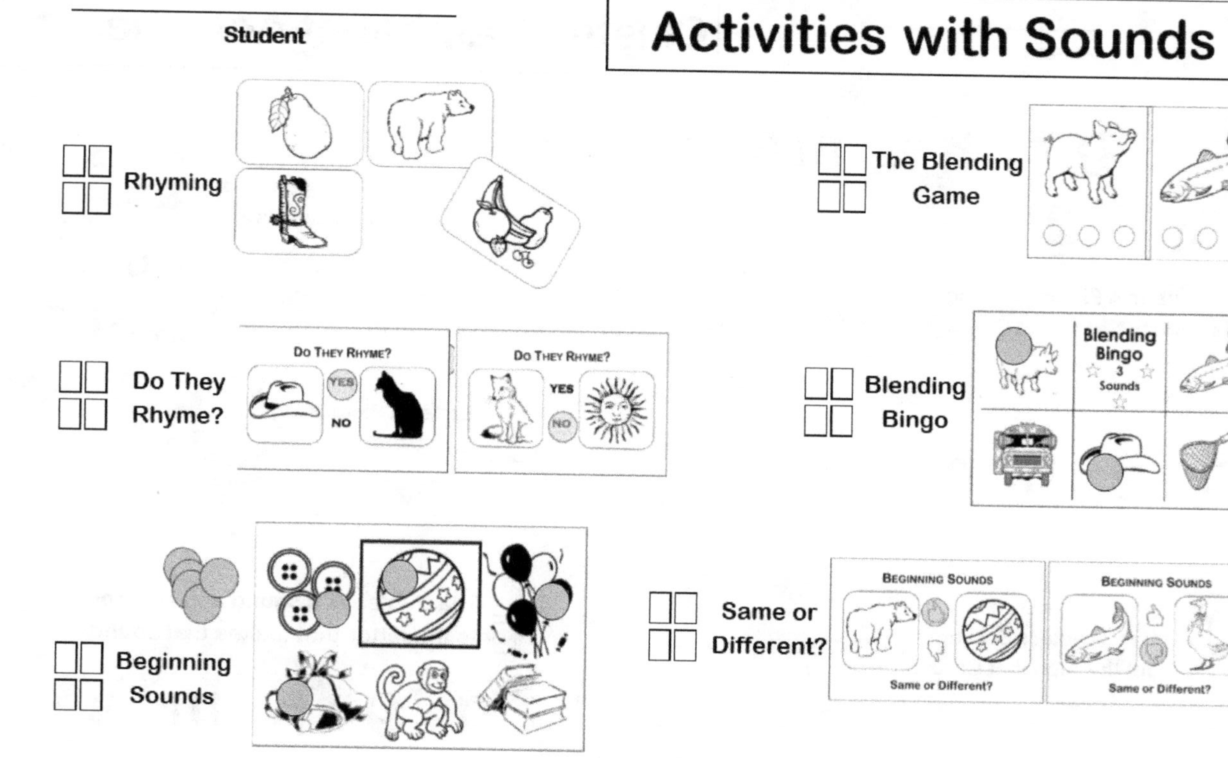
Activities with Sounds
Student
Rhyming
Do They Rhyme?
Do They Rhyme?
Yes
No
Do They Rhyme?
Yes
No
Beginning Sounds
The Blending Game
Blending Bingo
Blending Bingo
3
Sounds
Same or Different?
Beginning Sounds
Same or Different?
Beginning Sounds
Same or Different?

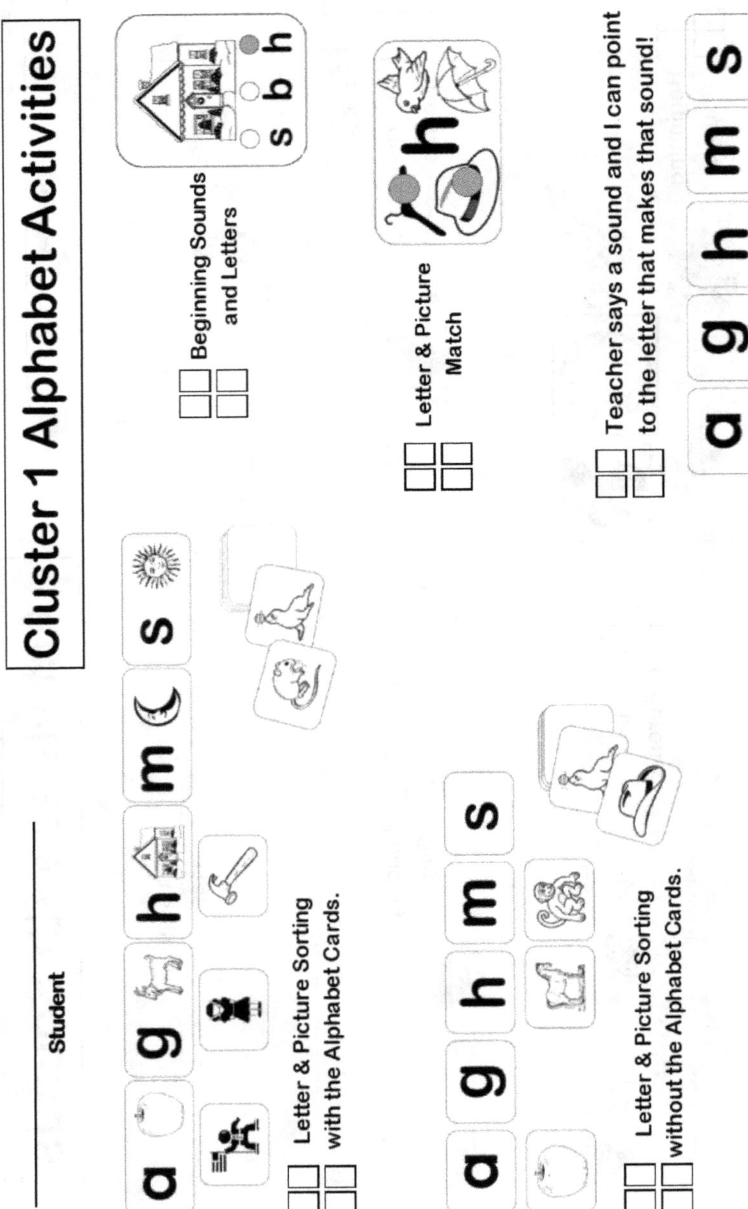
Cluster 1 Alphabet Activities
Student
s b h
Beginning Sounds and Letters
h
Letter & Picture Match
Teacher says a sound and I can point to the letter that makes that sound!
a g h m s
a g h m s
Letter & Picture Sorting with the Alphabet Cards.
a g h m s
Letter & Picture Sorting without the Alphabet Cards.

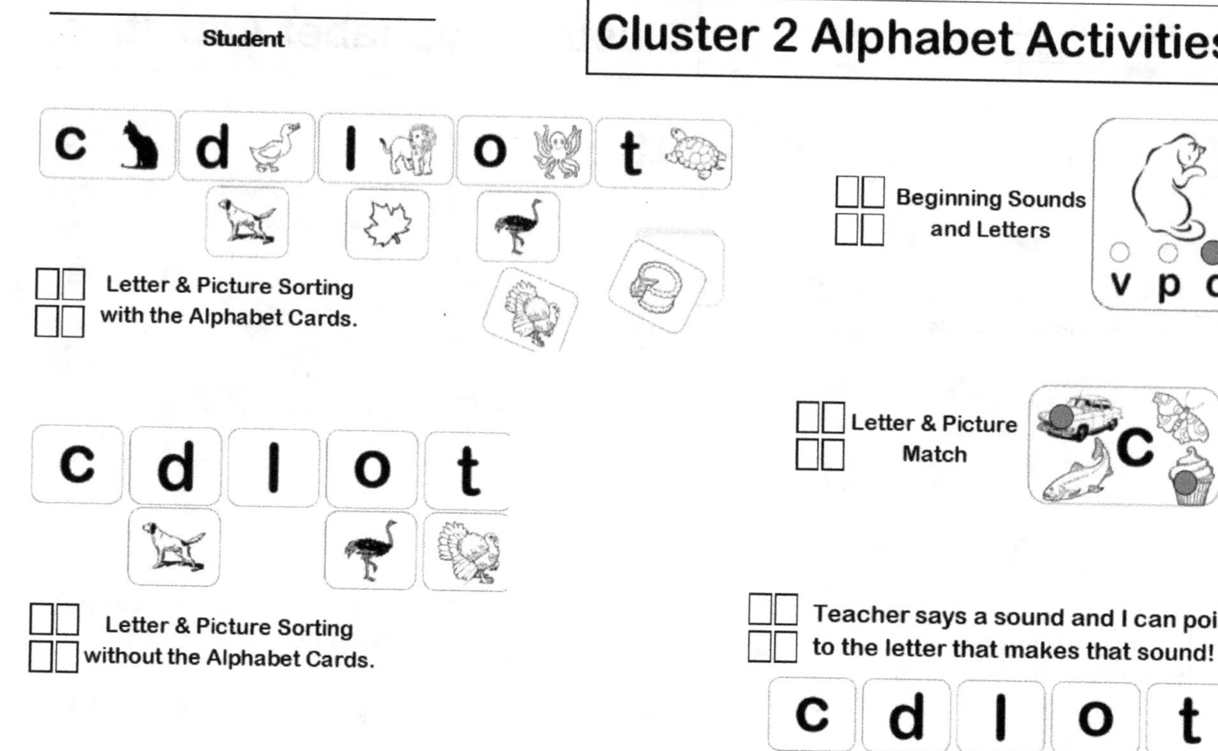
Student
Cluster 2 Alphabet Activities
c d l o t
Letter & Picture Sorting with the Alphabet Cards.
Beginning Sounds and Letters
v p c
Letter & Picture Match
c
c d l o t
Letter & Picture Sorting without the Alphabet Cards.
Teacher says a sound and I can point to the letter that makes that sound!
c d l o t

Cluster 3 Alphabet Activities

____
Student

f i p r u

☐☐ Letter & Picture Sorting with the Alphabet Cards.

f i p r u

☐☐ Letter & Picture Sorting without the Alphabet Cards.

☐☐ Beginning Sounds and Letters

p h e

☐☐ Letter & Picture Match

f

☐☐ Teacher says a sound and I can point to the letter that makes that sound!

f i p r u

Cluster 4 Alphabet Activities

Student ______________________

☐☐ Letter & Picture Sorting
☐☐ with the Alphabet Cards.

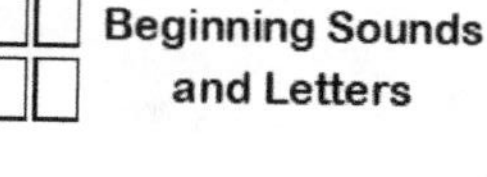

☐☐ Beginning Sounds
☐☐ and Letters

☐☐ Letter & Picture Sorting
☐☐ without the Alphabet Cards.

☐☐ Letter & Picture
☐☐ Match

☐☐ Teacher says a sound and I can point
☐☐ to the letter that makes that sound!

e j k n w

Cluster 5 Alphabet Activities

Student

b v y z qu

Letter & Picture Sorting with the Alphabet Cards.

b v y z qu

Letter & Picture Sorting without the Alphabet Cards.

Beginning Sounds and Letters

a b w

Letter & Picture Match

b

Teacher says a sound and I can point to the letter that makes that sound!

b v y z qu

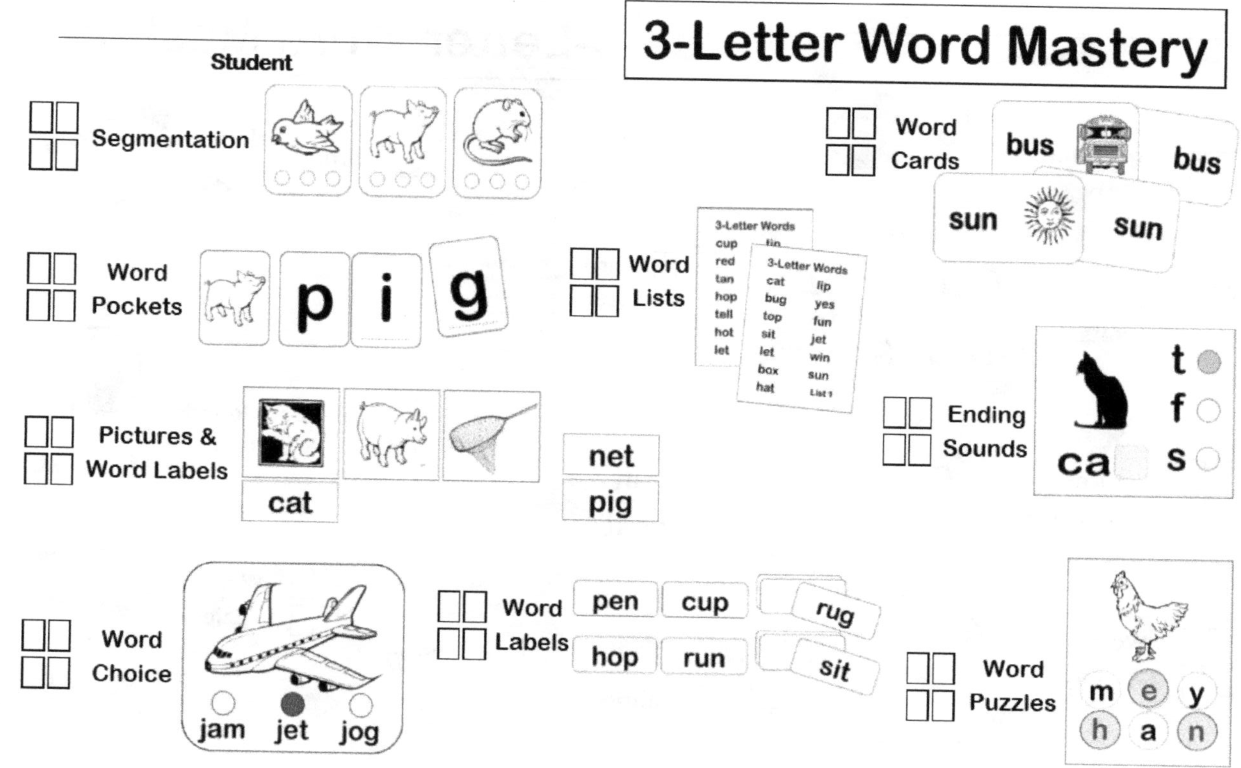
3-Letter Word Mastery
Student
Segmentation
Word Pockets
p i g
Pictures & Word Labels
cat
net
pig
Word Choice
jam jet jog
Word Cards
bus
bus
sun
sun
Word Lists
3-Letter Words
cup red tan hop tell hot let
3-Letter Words
cat bug top sit let box hat
lip yes fun jet win sun
List 1
Word Labels
pen
cup
hop
run
rug
sit
Ending Sounds
ca
t
f
s
Word Puzzles
m e y
h a n

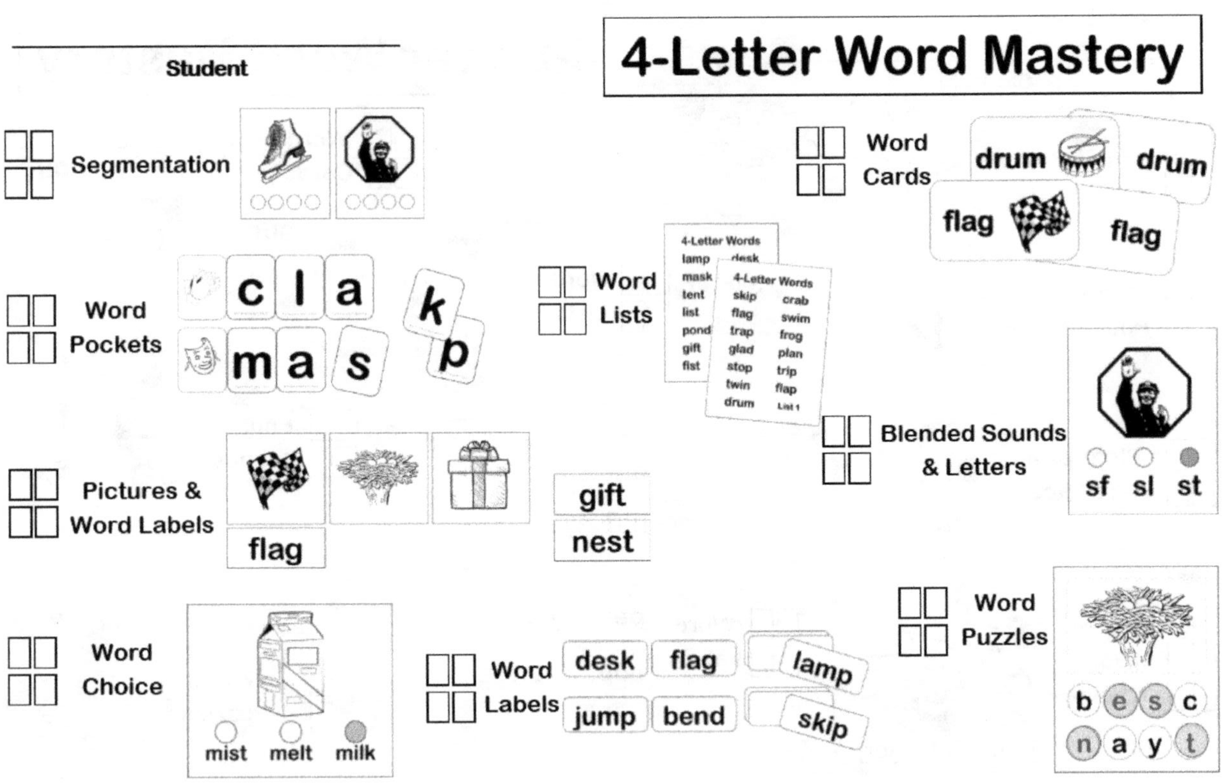
4-Letter Word Mastery
Student
Segmentation
Word Cards
drum
drum
flag
flag
Word Pockets
c l a
m a s
k
p
Word Lists
4-Letter Words
lamp desk
mask tent list pond gift fist
4-Letter Words
skip flag trap glad stop twin drum
crab swim frog plan trip flap
List 1
Blended Sounds & Letters
sf sl st
Pictures & Word Labels
flag
gift
nest
Word Choice
mist melt milk
Word Labels
desk flag
jump bend
lamp
skip
Word Puzzles
b e s c
n a y t

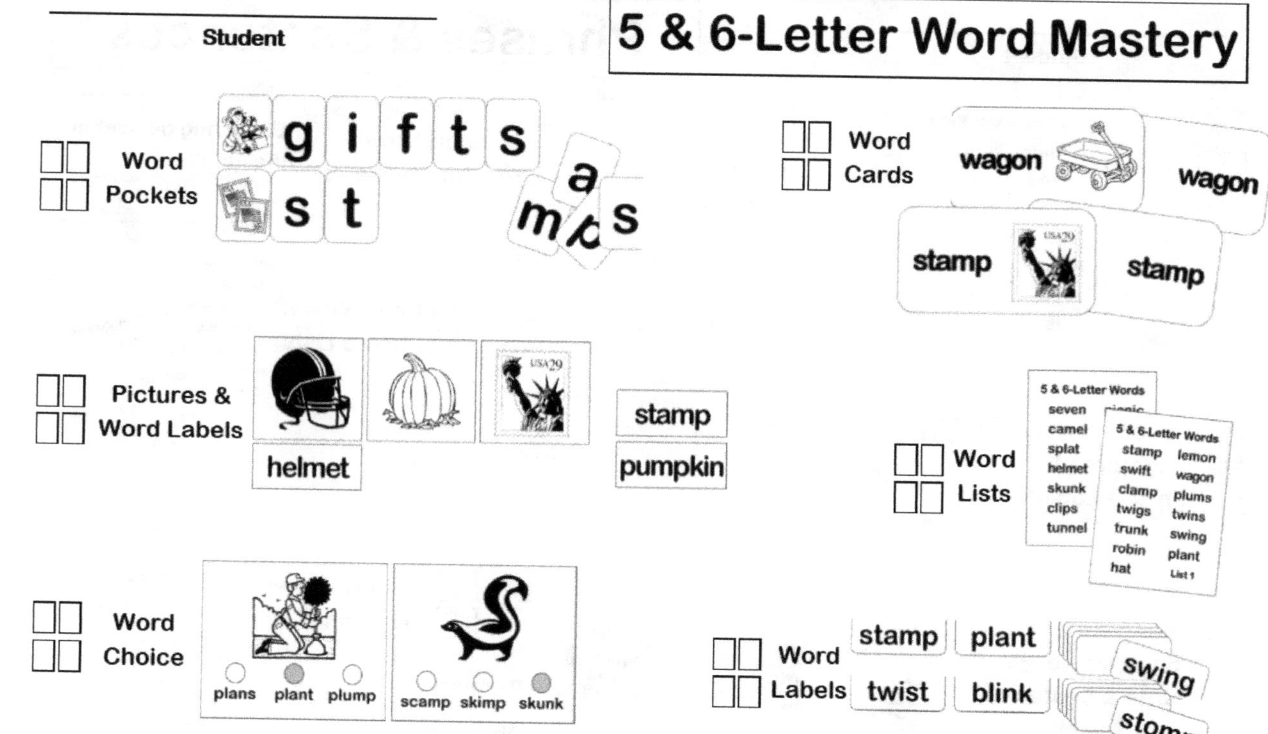
Student
5 & 6-Letter Word Mastery
Word Pockets
g i f t s
s t
a
m
s
Word Cards
wagon
wagon
stamp
stamp
Pictures & Word Labels
helmet
stamp
pumpkin
Word Lists
5 & 6-Letter Words
seven
camel
splat
helmet
skunk
clips
tunnel
5 & 6-Letter Words
stamp lemon
swift wagon
clamp plums
twigs twins
trunk swing
robin plant
hat
List 1
Word Choice
plans plant plump
scamp skimp skunk
Word Labels
stamp plant
twist blink
swing
stomp

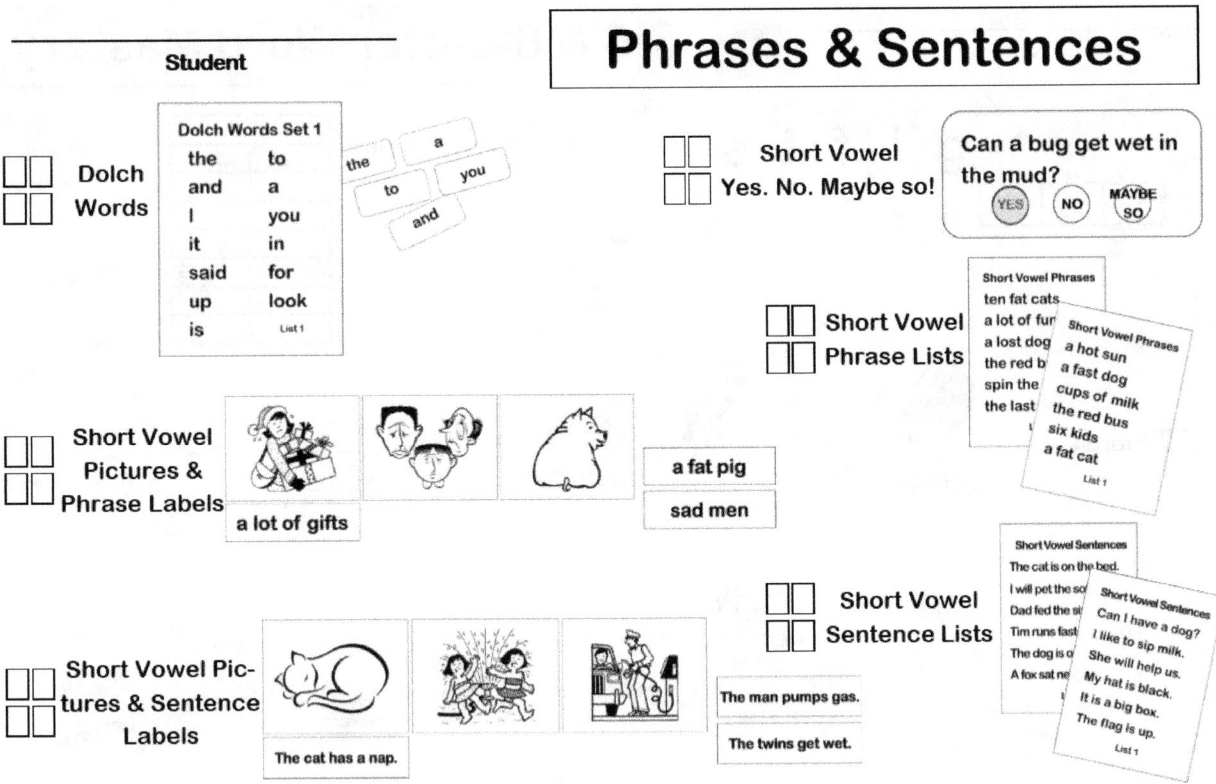
Phrases & Sentences
Student
Dolch Words
Dolch Words Set 1
the to
and a
I you
it in
said for
up look
is
List 1
the
a
to
you
and
Short Vowel
Yes. No. Maybe so!
Can a bug get wet in the mud?
YES
NO
MAYBE SO
Short Vowel Phrase Lists
Short Vowel Phrases
ten fat cats
Short Vowel Phrases
a hot sun
a fast dog
cups of milk
the red bus
six kids
a fat cat
List 1
Short Vowel Pictures & Phrase Labels
a lot of gifts
a fat pig
sad men
Short Vowel Sentence Lists
Short Vowel Sentences
The cat is on the bed.
Short Vowel Sentences
Can I have a dog?
I like to sip milk.
She will help us.
My hat is black.
It is a big box.
The flag is up.
List 1
Short Vowel Pictures & Sentence Labels
The cat has a nap.
The man pumps gas.
The twins get wet.

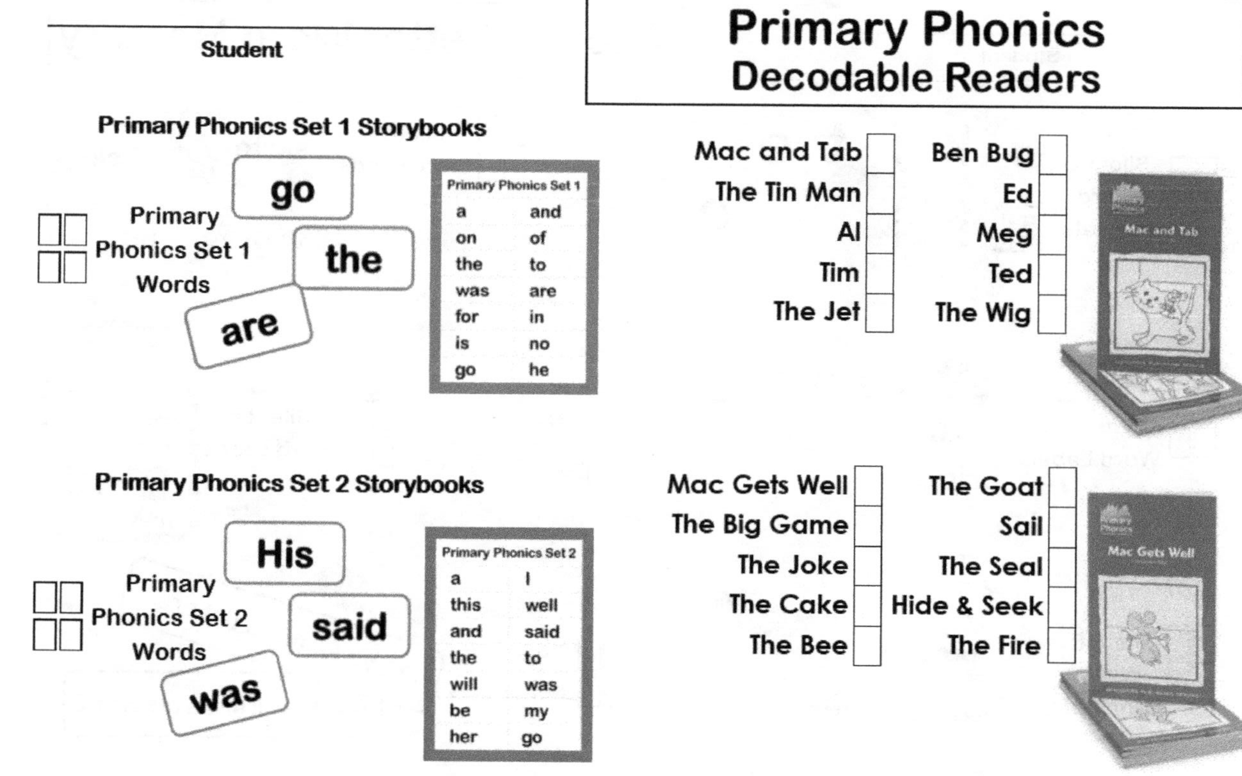
Student
Primary Phonics Set 1 Storybooks
Primary Phonics Set 1 Words
go
the
are
Primary Phonics Set 1
a and
on of
the to
was are
for in
is no
go he
Primary Phonics Set 2 Storybooks
Primary Phonics Set 2 Words
His
said
was
Primary Phonics Set 2
a I
this well
and said
the to
will was
be my
her go
Primary Phonics
Decodable Readers
Mac and Tab
The Tin Man
Al
Tim
The Jet
Ben Bug
Ed
Meg
Ted
The Wig
Mac and Tab
Mac Gets Well
The Big Game
The Joke
The Cake
The Bee
The Goat
Sail
The Seal
Hide & Seek
The Fire
Mac Gets Well

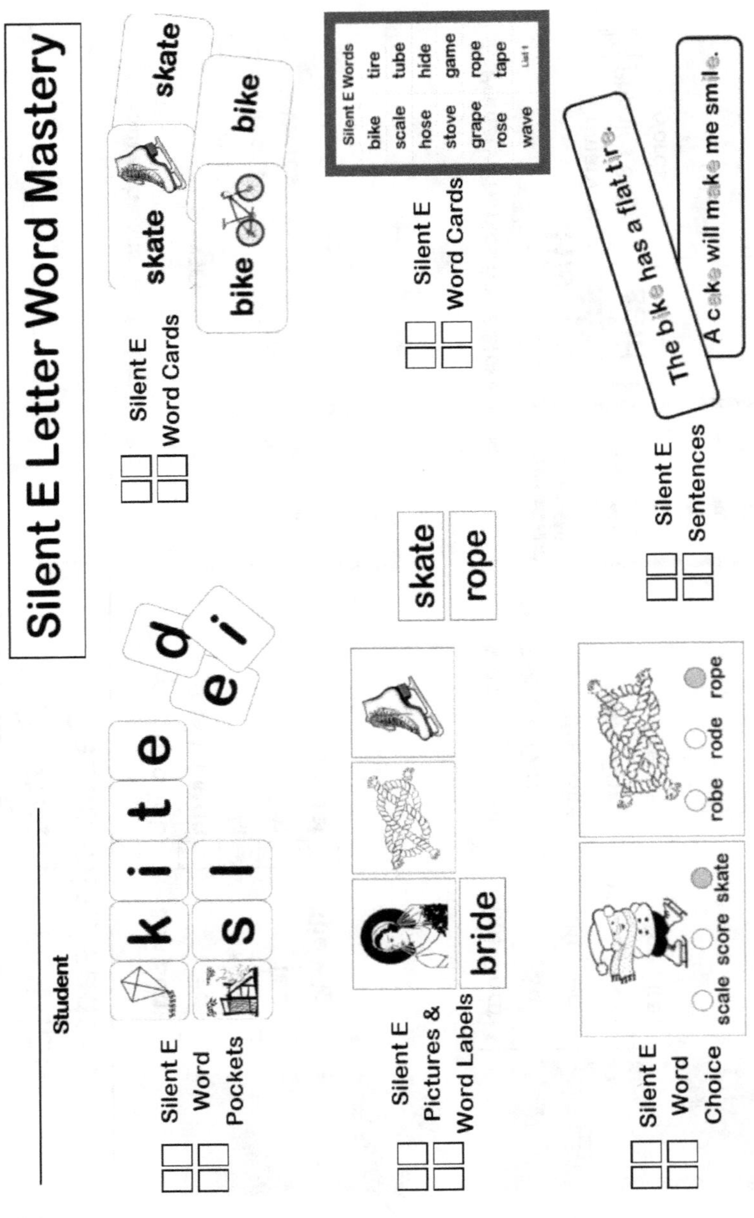
Silent E Letter Word Mastery
Student
Silent E Word Pockets
k i t e
s l
d e i
Silent E Pictures & Word Labels
bride
skate
rope
Silent E Word Choice
scale score skate
robe rode rope
Silent E Word Cards
skate
skate
bike
bike
Silent E Word Cards
Silent E Words
bike tire
scale tube
hose hide
stove game
grape rope
rose tape
wave
Silent E Sentences
The bike has a flat tire.
A cake will make me smile.

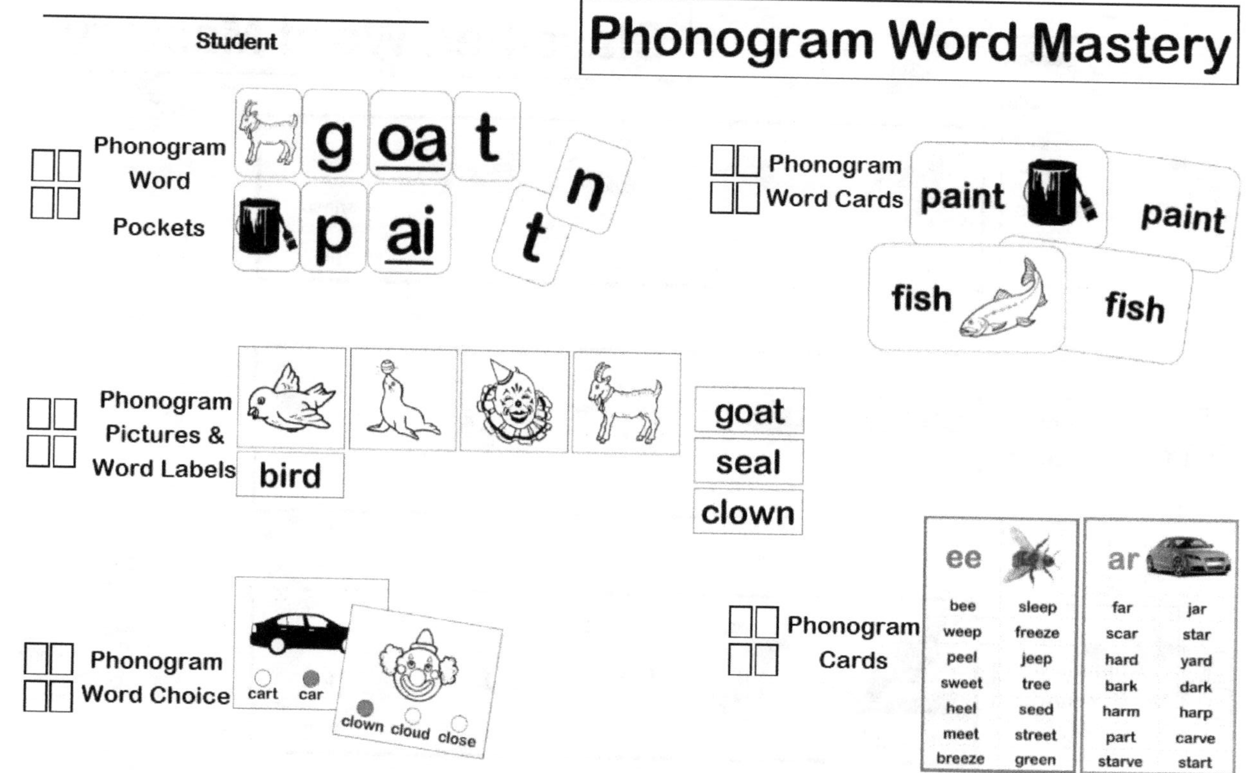

Student
Phonogram Word Mastery
Phonogram Word Pockets
g oa t
p ai
t
n
Phonogram Word Cards
paint
paint
fish
fish
Phonogram Pictures & Word Labels
bird
goat
seal
clown
Phonogram Word Choice
cart
car
clown
cloud
close
Phonogram Cards
ee
bee sleep
weep freeze
peel jeep
sweet tree
heel seed
meet street
breeze green
ar
far jar
scar star
hard yard
bark dark
harm harp
part carve
starve start

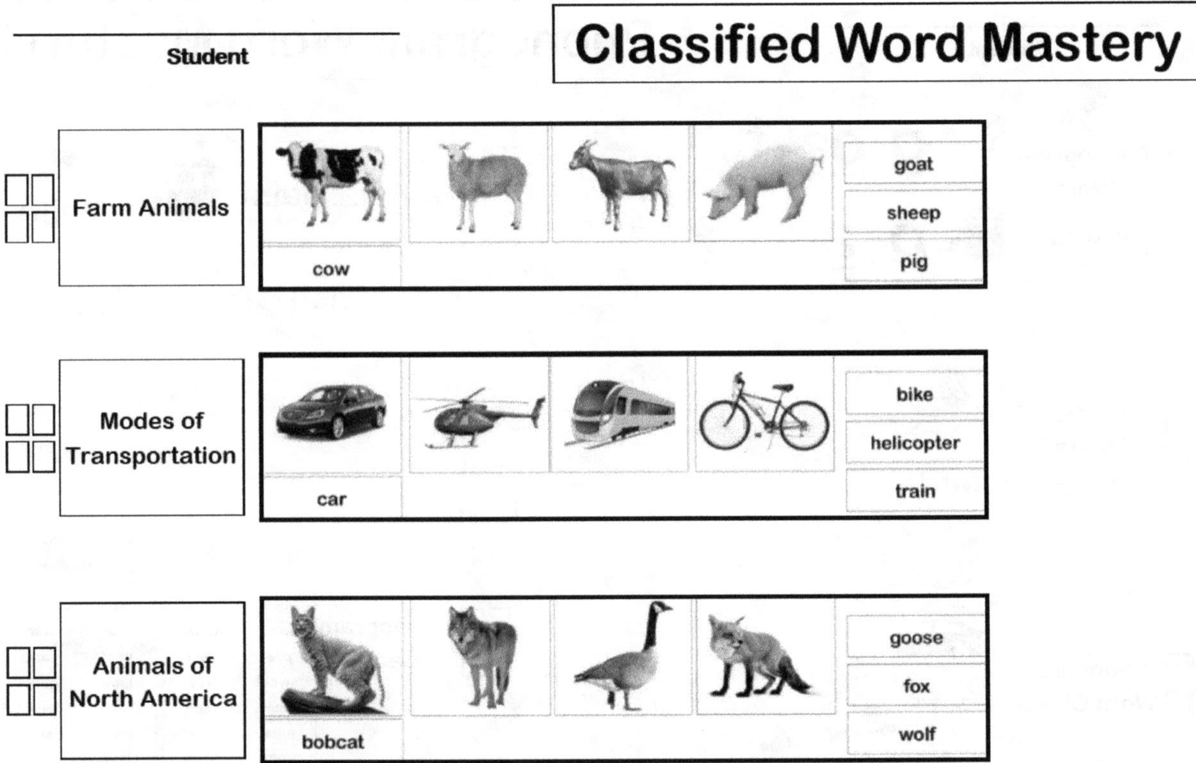
Classified Word Mastery
Student
Farm Animals
cow
goat
sheep
pig
Modes of Transportation
car
bike
helicopter
train
Animals of North America
bobcat
goose
fox
wolf

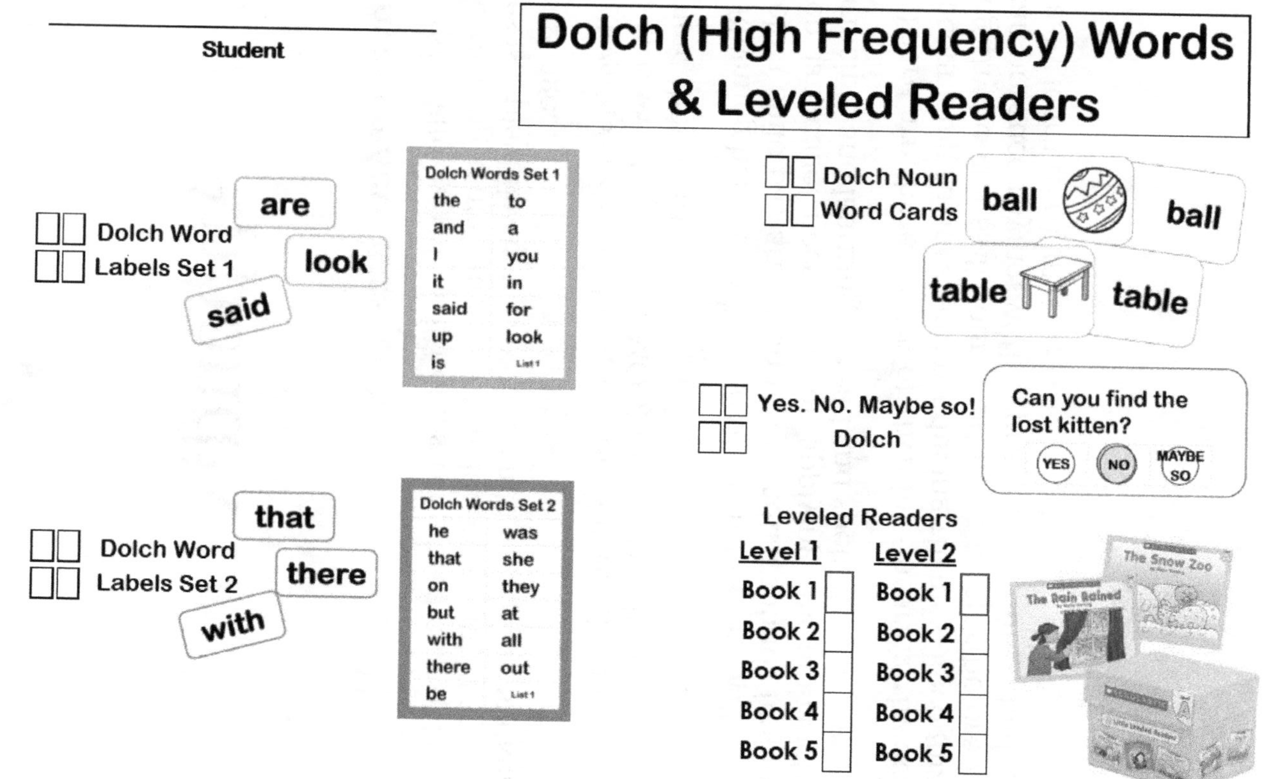
Student
Dolch (High Frequency) Words
& Leveled Readers
Dolch Word
Labels Set 1
are
look
said
Dolch Words Set 1
the to
and a
I you
it in
said for
up look
is
List 1
Dolch Word
Labels Set 2
that
there
with
Dolch Words Set 2
he was
that she
on they
but at
with all
there out
be
List 1
Dolch Noun
Word Cards
ball
ball
table
table
Yes. No. Maybe so!
Dolch
Can you find the lost kitten?
YES
NO
MAYBE SO
Leveled Readers
Level 1
Book 1
Book 2
Book 3
Book 4
Book 5
Level 2
Book 1
Book 2
Book 3
Book 4
Book 5
The Snow Zoo

Appendix D

Rhyming Activities

The ability to rhyme is not a strong predictor of later reading achievement, but including rhyming activities is a playful way for a young child to explore spoken language.

Rhyming focuses the attention not on the *meaning* of two words (HOUSE-MOUSE), but on the *chunks of sound* they share.

Rhyming helps to build neural pathways that will later help a child pay attention to individual sounds in spoken language, necessary for applying the alphabetic principle and learning to read and spell.

There are three stages of rhyming—hearing rhymes, recognizing rhymes, and producing rhymes. Recognizing rhyme is a skill your child must master before he can produce rhyme. With repeated exposure, children easily learn to rhyme.

Teach Rhyming Words
Item #100 [Large]

Purpose:

- To teach rhyming words
- To prepare students to identify rhymes
- To prepare students to rhyme independently

Activity:

1. Divide the pictures into smaller sets.
2. Choose one of the sets and introduce the vocabulary of the pictures to the students. As you flash the pictures and say the rhymes, have the children repeat the rhymes.

   Teacher: BEAR—PEAR
   Class: BEAR—PEAR
   Teacher: STAR—CAR
   Class: STAR—CAR

3. Continue flashing the rhyming cards and calling out the rhymes in this same manner each day.

4. The students soon become very familiar with the rhymes and you can begin to pause after each picture to give the students a chance to complete the rhyme.

   Teacher: BOX [PAUSE]
   Class: SOX!!
   Teacher: *Right!* BOX—SOX.

5. Each day more and more students will be calling out the correct rhyming word and soon this first set will be memorized by most of the students.

6. Now you can introduce the next set of rhyming pictures and continue in the manner described.

7. As each set of rhyming pictures is learned by the class, make it available for the students to work with independently. They can be shown to spread the cards out on a workspace and then match up the rhyming pictures as illustrated below.

Rhyming Pictures
Item #100 #101 [Small]

Purpose:

- Independent recognition of rhymes
- Independent practice for students who can already rhyme

Activity:

1. Place the game cards in an orderly manner on the right side of the workspace.
2. Choose a card, say the name of the picture and place it near the top of the workspace on the left side.
3. Search for the rhyming picture among the random cards.
4. Place the rhyming picture next to the first picture and say the rhyme, for example BEAR—PEAR.
5. Take another turn in order to model the process again.
6. Invite the student to have a turn and alternate turns as needed until he can work independently.
7. Show the student the image for this activity on the Activities with Sounds self-checking practice sheet.

Note: This material should be divided into smaller sets of approximately 8-10 rhyming pairs. Otherwise organizing them neatly on the workspace becomes too difficult.

Appendix E

Supplemental Letter Recognition Activities

Blended Sounds & Letters
Item #214

Purpose:

- Phoneme segmentation practice
- Practice separating two sounds that are "stuck together" in a blend
- Preparation for encoding and decoding 4-letter short vowel words

Activity:

1. Take a card from the stack that is placed facedown.
2. Identify the picture and segment the sounds.

STOP. /s/../t/../o/../p/.

3. Find the letters that match the first *two* sounds in the spoken word.

4. Invite the student to take a turn and alternate turns as needed.

Ending Sounds & Letters
Item #215

Purpose:

- Letter recognition practice
- Phoneme segmentation practice

Activity:

1. Segment the picture into three sounds in order to identify the ending sound, then put a game piece on the letter that matches that sound.

2. This game can be included in the 3-Letter Word Mastery activity cluster.

Middle Vowel Sounds & Letters
Item #216

Purpose:

- Letter recognition practice
- Phoneme segmentation practice

Activity:

1. Segment the picture into three sounds in order to identify the middle sound, then put a game piece on the letter that matches that sound.
2. This game can be included in the 3-Letter Word Mastery activity cluster.
3. This activity is very helpful in reinforcing the sounds of the five short vowels, which are often read incorrectly by beginning and struggling readers.

Middle Vowel Sorting
Item #217

Purpose:

- Focus on the five short vowel sounds
- Phoneme segmentation practice

Activity:

1. Segment the picture into three sounds in order to identify the middle sound, then place the picture card beneath the correct short vowel.
2. This game can be included in the 3-Letter Word Mastery activity cluster.
3. This activity is very helpful in reinforcing the sounds of the five short vowels, which are often read incorrectly by beginning and struggling readers.

Appendix F

High Frequency (Dolch) Words

The following is a list of the 100 most frequent words in the English language. These first 100 words make up approximately 50% of everything grade school children will read.

Every student must be taught these words systematically over the weeks and months of reading instruction. This should begin after the student has achieved success decoding short vowel words and is ready to read phrases and sentences.

Automatic recognition of these high frequency sight words together with knowledge of basic phonics and strong decoding skill form the foundations of reading success.

the →	to	and	he	a	I	you	it	of
in	was	said	this	that	she	for	on	they
but	had	at	him	with	up	all	look	is
her	there	some	out	as	be	have	go	we
am	then	little	down	do	can	could	when	did
what	so	see	not	were	get	them	like	one
this	my	would	me	will	yes	big	went	are
come	if	now	long	no	came	ask	very	an
over	your	its	rid	into	just	blue	red	from
good	any	about	aroun d	want	don't	how	know	right
put	too	got	take	where	every	pretty	jump	green
four								

Appendix G

Early Reading Mastery Literacy Centers

- Churches, civic groups and charity organizations that work with disadvantaged populations and struggling learners will find this method of organizing early reading instruction easy to implement, primarily because it doesn't require extensive training for those who will be guiding the children.
- This program is appropriate for children ages 3-7. An 8- or 9-year-old child who has some dropped stitches in decoding and word identification will also benefit from this program and will move through the lessons quickly, gaining mastery and confidence along the way.
- Children are not taught in groups but work independently or with other students.
- There is no need for elaborate testing or evaluations prior to starting a child in the program.
- Some children will need to spend time with instructors to learn how to isolate beginning sounds of spoken words. Beginning sound isolation is the only skill that is needed to begin independent work with activities that teach the sounds of the alphabet A-Z.

- Some children will need to spend time with instructors to learn how to segment spoken words into individual sounds (phonemes). Phoneme segmentation is the only skill that is needed to begin independent work with the activities that teach children how to decode words.
- Once the instructor teaches a student an activity, the student is free to choose that activity during practice sessions. Independence and freedom of choice are fundamental to the success of this method of early reading mastery. We empower children to teach themselves and to share in the responsibility for their own learning.
- Games are organized in easy-to-identify activity clusters. Each cluster matches a specific skill or set of skills that is required to play those games.
- Children are given self-checking practice sheets which guide them through the sequences of alphabet and decoding activities. They learn to share in the responsibility for their own learning and choose appropriate activities during practice sessions. They learn to track their own progress.
- The instructor's role is to supervise practice and give assistance to children who may be struggling and to take note of those who are ready to graduate to the next level of challenge.

For more information about starting an Early Reading Literacy Center contact:

Randall Klein
P.O. Box 10935
Bozeman Montana 59719 USA
+1 800-890-1961
earlyreadingmastery@gmail.com
www.earlyreadingmastery.com

What Teachers and Parents Say About the Klein Method

The Klein Method was a huge success in my preschool classroom for over a decade. My students flocked to the Klein materials. Year after year I saw young children naturally and with great pleasure teach themselves to read.

J. A., Retired preschool teacher and grandmother

Randall Klein's early reading materials were the pillars of our Fun Way Learning Center tutoring program for over 15 years. His abundance of hands-on materials has provided hundreds of children "just the right lessons" for success and steady growth.

Lydia Widmer, Newburyport MA

Randall teaches his method of early reading instruction to students in my elementary teacher training program. These adult learners gain a profound understanding of teaching reading to young children.

Janet Nordemann

Randall Klein's methods are fantastic! At our Montessori school all children from ages 3 to 6 years learn to read with the Klein Method materials. Every child in our school learns to read before entering kindergarten.

Constance Dratz, Preschool and elementary school director

I am a Special Needs teacher in London and have been following Randall Klein for some time. The Klein Method games and activities have been ideal for my struggling learners. Thank you, Randall! I am so grateful.

Miss Ali, London, UK

Randall Klein's Early Reading Mastery methods have enriched my teaching methods for almost twenty years. They have had the greatest impact on my students' learning and success.

Tondi Petersen, Kindergarten Teacher

I am delighted with Randall Klein's materials and use them daily in my Montessori classroom. The students are attracted to the materials and choose to work with them regularly. I cannot imagine my language shelves without them!

Patricia Patrick, Maple Ridge, B.C. Canada

The Klein Method has totally transformed the way I approach reading instruction in my classroom. I now have the tools that I need to identify exactly where my struggling readers are getting stuck and how to help them.

Amy A., Montessori Lower Elementary Teacher

Our family has played Randall's reading games with our grandchildren to help them learn how to read. The games are fun and easy to play and we all have a great time together.

Kathryn L., Grandmother

The Klein Method materials are foundational to any reading instruction program and can also be used effectively by homeschooling parents and reading tutors. With these materials the child internalizes reading skills while gaining confidence in himself.

Jo-Anne Woodland, Reading Tutor, retired Montessori Teacher

As a reading specialist I have found The Klein Method to be the most straightforward and easy-to-use materials. Our reading intervention program has been strengthened by use of these methods and materials.

Kaylene Redd, Reading Specialist, Kaysville Utah

The Randall Klein Early Reading Mastery Method is amazing. It is playful, child friendly and intuitive for young children. The Klein method is unique and can be applied successfully on any continent around the world.

Marius van Dorp, Principal (retired), Lanto Montessori Schools, South Africa.

The Klein Method games and activities are some of the most engaging and fun ways for children to practice reading skills that I have found.

Tevia Arlidge
Lower Elementary Teacher, Montessori School of Maui

For more information about the methods and materials described in this book or to schedule an in-person or virtual Early Reading Mastery presentation contact:

Randall Klein
P.O. Box 10935
Bozeman Montana USA 59719
+1-800-890-1961

earlyreadingmastery@gmail.com
www.earlyreadingmastery.com